365 Ways

to Bless

Your Wife

365 Ways

to Bless

Your Wife

Glenn Egli & Jennifer Carrell

BRIDGE PUBLISHING
South Plainfield, NJ

365 Ways to Bless Your Wife
   by Glenn Egli and Jennifer Carrell
ISBN 0-88270-665-9
Library of Congress Catalog Card #94-070065
Copyright © 1994 by Glenn Egli and Jennifer Carrell

Published by:
Bridge Publishing Inc.
2500 Hamilton Blvd.
South Plainfield, NJ 07080

To Ardis
and
to Dean....

And with gratitude to
the many women
whose expression of need
shaped this book.

Contents

Foreword

Billy Sunday's legacy of witticisms includes this advice: "Try praising your wife, even if it does frighten her at first." I suggested that to a friend once. His marriage was as flat as a forgotten glass of Coke. And no wonder. He was so hopelessly illiterate in the art of affirming that he spluttered back, "But what do I pick to praise her for?"

There's no need to worry about that now! In this little book by Glenn Egli and Jennifer Carrell, we men are not only encouraged to bless our wives but are given a year's worth of practical ways to do it.

What fun!

One Christmas, our family decided to bless a father and his two young daughters. For twelve nights we left anonymous gifts at their doorstep. After a few days, they tried hard to catch us, but we always outsmarted them. The next year we successfully completed the same goal with another family. But one morning after we had delivered a poinsettia, we learned they suspected us of being the conspirators. We huddled and decided on a diversionary tactic. That very day we brought them *another* poinsettia — this time in person! "We thought maybe you'd enjoy a little Christmas gift," we said. They were dumfounded. You could see their theory evaporate. From that moment on they suspected anybody else, *except us*, of delivering the secret gifts!

But if it's pleasurable to bless those outside your family, how much more delightful to bless those you love most! Husbands, remember the joy of bestowing little kindnesses when the two of you were still dating? Why not resurrect and cultivate those gestures? I guarantee you, it will be more fun than ever — even if, as Billy Sunday predicted, it *does* frighten her in the beginning.

If you're the rational-theological type and need biblical justification for such rash behavior, remember that God is in the blessing business. The cosmogonies of the ancient Near East were invented to bless and buttress the authority of tribal and national rulers. But, at Sinai, the one Creator God revealed himself as the God of all, whose purpose in creating us was to bless us all. He chose Abraham and Israel, not out of partisanship, but to bless all peoples (Genesis 12:3, 18:18, 22:18, 26:4). Israel's destiny was to be "light to the nations," showing the blessing of living under God's rule. So when Israel wanted a king "like other nations," the desire was granted only on condition that Israel and her king remain loyal, first of all, to God. Why? Because only by maintaining ultimate allegiance to God could Israel continue to show *the blessing* of living for God. The theme continues in the Psalms (72:17) and the prophets (Isaiah 45:22). In Jeremiah 4:2, the renewed blessing of the nations depends on Israel's repentance and return to God.

As you would expect, the same thread weaves through the New Testament. The communion cup is a "cup of blessing" (1 Corinthians 10:16). The good news we share is for the blessing of *ta ethne*, "the peoples" (Matthew 24:24; 28:19). In making disciples we not only bless them (Acts 3:26), but put them on the path to the ultimate blessing (Revelation 22:2).

The point is that, as God is in the blessing business (Hebrews 6:14), so He wants us to be in the blessing business. And if so... if we are to bless even those who curse us and persecute us (Luke 6:28; Romans 12:14; 1 Corinthians 4:12), how much more ought we to bless those we love most!

Two things Glenn and Jennifer don't tell you about this little book.... First, if you will follow it for even six to eight weeks, it will become habitual. And, when that happens, your marriage will be enriched immensely in an ongoing and cumulative way. Second, as you bless your wife, you'll learn to bless additional persons, enriching other relationships. And, third, as you bless your wife, guess who also gets blessed? That's right — *you*!

If you are someone's husband, you need this book. Take it to the cashier and purchase it now. Better still, buy an extra copy for a friend and bless him, too. Believe me, you'll never make a better investment!

Art McPhee

Authors' Note

In making his or her way through these pages, the reader will notice that references to the Holy Spirit will appear without the article "the." The authors explain:

"Holy Spirit is the personal name of the Third Person of the Trinity. In the original Greek language, the article 'the' used before Holy Spirit is often omitted. In the English language, when referring to God, we do not say or write 'the' God or 'the' Jesus. Therefore, we think it is disrespectful to say or write 'the' Holy Spirit."

Glenn Egli
Jennifer Carrell

Introduction

So what's this "blessing" thing, anyway?

This book began as a collection of illustrations and ideas to defeat a growing phenomenon—failed marriages. As husbands and wives entered Glenn's office for counseling and discipling, a clear pattern emerged. Most marriages weren't crashing and burning, they were dying over a period of years from indifference, neglect, and even ignorance. Both of us have friends and colleagues who describe their marriage as empty and meaningless—somehow the passion and joy have disappeared. We believe God has an answer!

Throughout the Bible, God uses the act of *blessing* to restore hope and life. A blessing is any good gift that gives a positive benefit. God uses blessing to meet our needs. The concept and practice of blessing accurately describes the missing element in many marriage relationships where needs often remain unmet. 1 Peter 3:8-9 reveals the importance of blessing for everyone who follows Christ: "Finally, all of you, live in harmony with one another; be sympathetic, love as brothers, be compassionate and humble. Do not repay evil with evil or insult with insult, but with *blessing* because to this you were called so that you may inherit a *blessing.*"

First, this scripture says we are called to bless. Second, it says if we bless, we will inherit blessings. (Of course, it also implies that if we curse, we will inherit curses!) Blessing your wife is much like praying to God. It benefits you as much as it benefits your wife. As a husband, you need to know that 1 Peter 3:8-9 is a covenant between you and God. This promise ensures that if you bless your wife—with kind words, thoughtful actions and prayer—you will receive blessings in return. When God asks you to accomplish something, He also promises to help you accomplish it. And God keeps His Word!

In the following pages you will discover personal stories that illustrate over 70 different topics, each accompanied by five specific ways to bless your wife. Though each of these blessings are written from a woman's perspective, the stories relate events we have experienced individually. These 365 blessings are designed as practical applications to meet many of your wife's needs.

Physically—
> with tender touch, exotic dates, special gifts, mini-vacations or unusual romance...

> *Emotionally—*
>> with creative intimacy, tangible support, or unique expressions of love...

>> *and Spiritually—*
>>> with healing prayers and life-changing promises from God!

While some appear simple and others more complex, all of these blessings can be used to begin blessing your wife today and every day!

What Does Blessing Have To Do With Your Wife?

Blessing is about meeting needs. Many wives who seek marriage counseling repeatedly describe how their husbands fail to acknowledge or meet their needs. Listening to hurting wives, it becomes apparent that these women are often suffering from loneliness, abuse or neglect. They realize that their marriage is disintegrating, but sometimes their husbands are not aware. Over a period of time, distance grows between them, resulting from unmet needs.

We recorded specific needs these women shared and compiled a list of 200 in a few short days. Studying this problem and praying for answers, we learned that education provides a key to its solution. What these husbands don't realize about God's power—or know about their wives—may destroy their marriages.

These husbands aren't bad men. Many are simply unaware that their wives have unmet needs. If husbands are aware of needs, often they do not believe they have the ability to meet them. The fifth chapter of Ephesians tells us something quite different. It states that the relationship of marriage is designed to be like the relationship between Christ and the Church. Just as Christ meets the needs of the Church, husbands are equipped by God to meet the needs of their wives!

Jesus shows us the perfect example of blessing in His relationship with the disciples. He models blessing by meeting their physical, emotional, and spiritual needs—ministering to each of them as a whole person. In John 13:1, He reveals His intent to bless them at the passover meal: "...having loved his own who were in the world, he now showed them the full extent of his love." As a husband, your intent must be to show your wife the full extent of Christ's love!

How Does Blessing Work?

Blessing works much like an antibiotic. You may not understand how it works or you may not believe that it works at all. However, if you decide to take the medicine anyway, it will gradually make you well. You may not see any effects at first, but as you continue to follow the prescription three times each day for many days, healing will eventually occur. The healing power of blessing your wife is not a miracle of medicine. Rather, it is a miracle offered to us by God. We must decide either to ignore it or use it.

This biblical concept of blessing by meeting needs has been shared with many husbands. They and their wives are amazed at the healing that continually occurs. From experience they are finding that blessing by direct intent is God's idea, and that the practice of blessing makes marriage triumph in the midst of conflict!

Luke 6:38, provides a great picture of what this kind of blessing can bring: "Give, and it will be given to you. A good measure, pressed down, shaken together and running over, will be poured in your lap. For with the measure you use, it will be measured to you." Obviously, no one wins in a marriage relationship without blessing. It seems equally clear that good intentions alone do not heal relationships. Therefore, be the first to bless. Be the first to meet her needs. God has promised that He will meet all of yours! Your responsibility as a husband requires you to bless your wife unconditionally and to meet her needs. Her responsibility requires her to receive those blessings and respond by blessing you.

If your first reaction to these 365 blessings feels like guilt or despair, don't panic—God provides possibility! Since God calls you to bless your wife, He also commits to give you the resources and the ability. In Philippians 4:13, He tells us He will give us the strength to do anything He asks of us. (That makes a man of God an awesome husband!)

Blessing can be a simple act, but one filled with powerful love. For all of us, it holds a promise. For husbands, it provides reassurance that serving your wife can be as simple as praying over her, asking about her day, or holding her hand. God does the healing.

We encourage you to experience God's promise that He will empower you at this moment to meet your wife's physical, emotional, and spiritual needs. By blessing your wife with the ability God has given you, she can experience healing, and you will receive a blessing!

Glenn Egli & Jennifer Carrell

Physical Blessings

Romancing

There they were. Six young women dressed in white caps and uniforms, walking down the hall toward me. They were talking and laughing. Then I noticed...that walk. That distinctive cut of her hair. Suddenly, my heart felt like it was pushing into my throat!

Wait! She wasn't even going to notice me! I wanted to say, "hi!", but somehow my voice wouldn't cooperate.

What happened next was like lightning striking in the middle of a crashing Illinois thunderstorm . . . .

She was looking straight into my eyes. Her eyes lit up with a sparkle that made me feel like fainting, hugging her, and shouting—all at the same time! I felt like the most important person in the world!

But what was it? Whatever it was, it lit up all the lights on my board! My internal control panel was on overload. It was—awesome!

Some people call it romance. I don't know for sure what to call it. But I know this; it was not happening by default. It was happening by direct intent. She had an internal "sender switch" turned to "on," and I had an internal 'receiving switch' turned to 'on'!

Our spirits were making contact by direct intent. It was pure risk! I was risking to let her into my interior to know me.

Is your spirit—your sender *and* receiver—turned to "on"? Or is it jammed "off"? Risk! Romance her with direct intent. Perhaps the lightning of romance will light up her internal control panel!

G.E.

Blessings

1   Take her on a date. Hold her close, look into her eyes and send a romantic message!

2   Rent memorable movies, buy her favorite snack food and cuddle on the sofa for a few romantic hours.

3   Take a quiet boat or canoe ride at night. Bring music, and let her lean against you as you put your arms around her.

4   Remember your first date together? Is it worth repeating? Recreate it with food, music and location, if possible. Tell her what your impressions were on that occasion. (Fan the embers of romance!)

5   Invite her for a midnight walk to see the stars and look at God's world after dark.

Playing

I could hear a guy's voice rumbling in another room. Girls were laughing, and I didn't need much coaxing for a study break. Halfway down the hall, I intercepted "the voice" on his way out. He was a friend of a friend—I'd seen him before, usually heading down the hill toward soccer practice with cleats hanging over one shoulder. I considered him definitely out of reach. But today, he seemed genuinely friendly. . . .

The next thing I know—SLAM! A soccer ball smacked the wall beside me. I kicked it back—hard! Before I had time to think about being uncomfortable, we were throwing elbows, hacking shins and having a great time on our linoleum "field." A five-minute match!

We had a class together in the winter. We smiled at each other once in a while. Occasionally we studied together. Seriously. No talking, no snacks, no breaks, no kidding. But a midnight walk to the convenience store cut through any lingering formalities. The air stung our noses, and we nearly jogged back to the dorm to keep warm. Each blade of grass was stiff with flakes of frost—too slick to resist. We ran as hard as we could, then skidded and slid, making shiny green tracks across the lawn. It was kid-like—just for kicks. It was fun to think of it together.

A year later, he said he thought he liked me. We did all the usual dating stuff—eating out, staying up late, dancing, etc.. But we kind of toyed with crazy ideas, too. One Friday night seemed especially dull, so we decided to dress up. A trip to the drugstore netted a can of spray hair dye (removable via shampoo). In fifteen minutes, we both had jet-black hair, and in ten minutes more, we had begged and borrowed enough leather and accessories to "go punk." We must have been convincing, because it felt like being in someone else's skin for a while.

When was the last time you were "someone else"? Try it! Be relaxed with your wife, be kids together. Learn to play!

J.C.

Blessings

6   Play outside. Hide and seek? (Hide a special gift and let her look for it.) In the snow? (Double-decker inner-tubing!)

7   Play for keeps. Chess? (Each captured chessman is exchanged for a kiss.)

8   Play in the car. "I'm thinking of _____" (All the reasons you love her).

9   Play risky. Truth or dare? (With all sorts of consequences!)

10   Play at night. (Strip backgammon?)

Touching

Have you ever felt like you just needed some warm skin against you?

An embolism had just lodged in my brain. I lay on a hard table in the cold emergency room. When a nurse put her warm hand on my arm, my whole body and spirit were warmed! Touch. How important is it?

The Bible says that people "were pushing forward to touch Him [Jesus]" (Mark 3:10). Why? They knew there was healing power in touching. People can touch with the intent of blessing or evil. Think of the Voodoo witch doctors. They also wish to touch—sometimes with curses! The effect is determined by the intent of the human spirit!

Jesus knew touch was important. Through His touch, blind eyes were healed, lepers were cleansed, sickness departed and people rose up to serve Him!

Is there a wound in your spouse that needs to be healed? Perhaps she simply needs to be surprised by a touch of divine love! By direct intent (choosing) and exercised faith, you can touch your spouse with divine empowering. You will never know the power of divine touch unless you try.

Press forward right now with the direct intent for Christ to touch her!

G.E.

Blessings

11   After a tiring day, wash her feet in warm water and rub them with lotion.

12   Hold her hand in church. (In Genesis 26:8, Isaac caresses Rebekah, a sign to everyone that she was his wife.) *Heavenly Father, help me to remember Genesis 26:8, and to show affection to my wife when we're in public.*

13   In the evening—turn off all the lights except a few candles or the fireplace, and hold her on your lap in a rocking chair.

14   Gently and softly massage her forehead, jaw and cheekbones. (Make sure you have at least fifteen minutes in a quiet, dimly lit room.)

15   Visit a cosmetics counter together. Find a product that custom-blends lotions and soaps. Choose a combination of scents you both like, and give her a full body rub when you get home!

Reading

The sun was peeking over the horizon. My morning jog. I noted my neighbors, a couple sitting on their deck. He was reading a book. Not that unusual. But something was. He was reading out loud and his wife was listening!

I finished my morning jog and they were still on the deck. He was still reading and she was still listening! My curiosity simply overcame me.

"Hey, John, what are you doing?" I called.

"I'm reading with and to my wife—*The Screwtape Letters*—ever hear of it?"

"Sure, that book is a classic. Tell me something Beth; does John read to you often?"

"Yes," she replied, "and I love it!"

I was intrigued. "Why do you love it when John reads to you?"

"Do you remember that John had a heart attack three years ago? Ever since then, I have just loved to hear his voice. It is so comforting. It is a reminder of his healing. I am so thankful. And he picks such good books. I feel that John respects my intellect and my ability to understand. His respect is so important to me."

She put her face between her hands. "I used to think John was so boring and lazy. Then he started reading to me. Why he is a downright interesting man, a real thinker!"

She hesitated, then continued. "And just the fact that he wants me to be with him during these early morning times is so precious—Oh!" She spoke with a start. "One other thing. It gives me respect for him as a spiritual leader. And that is most important!"

I looked at John with a grin. "Wow, those are big dividends for reading books out loud. From boring and lazy to a downright interesting thinker and spiritual leader! I wonder if it would do that for me?" John had a twinkle in his eye. A slow grin spread across his face as he picked up his book again. "You'll never know unless you try!"

Neither will you.

G.F.

Blessings

16   Plan an indoor picnic with finger food and no dishes to clean. Sit in front of the fireplace and let her relax as you read aloud. (Psalms? Agatha Christie? Dave Barry? Mother Goose? Tolstoy?)

17   Read her body language! (Learn to recognize when she is tired, anxious, joyful or needing affection.)

18   Read the Bible aloud to her. (Hold her in bed and read the passionate words in The Song of Songs.)

19   Pick one night each week to read aloud to her and/or your children. (*The Chronicles of Narnia* series, by C.S. Lewis, are excellent for a variety of ages!)

20   Be a news anchor on Saturday mornings. Read the paper to her as you linger over breakfast— or later in the day, after the kids are *supposed* to be napping.

Giving

It was my birthday. And it was no big deal in my rural, Mennonite family. Gifts were few and birthday parties didn't exist. But I can remember it like it was yesterday. I was eighteen that day.

My brother was two years older than me. I wanted to be like him. He was happy, fun, good-looking and popular. He also became engaged that spring. And suddenly, like something out of nothing, he and his fiancee gave me a sport shirt for my birthday! No one in the world could have been more surprised than I was. A present, just for me! Just because I was me!

I remember it well. It was a green sport shirt! I wore it everywhere. I told everyone it was a gift from my brother. I wore it like an Olympic medal, because it meant more to me to me than any medal could have. When it was completely worn out, I carried it in the trunk of my car. For years, I used it to put the final shine on my car. It matched the shine in my heart! Today, the green sport shirt is no longer on my back or in my trunk. But it is in my heart forever.

Jesus liked gifts. He gave His life as a gift to us. I guess He thought that giving such a gift would be too big for us to start with, so He said, "Start with a cup of cold water"—or maybe a green sport shirt!

Give her a gift today.

Maybe it will end up in her heart forever!

G.E.

Blessings

21   Treat her to a small accessory (scarf, earrings, hat, bracelet, pin, etc.) before a special occasion.

22   Arrange for each of her friends to bring a single rose to her on her birthday. (You provide the vase!)

23   Hide clues around the house to lead her to a new book or a bottle of perfume.

24   Buy her a handmade sweater in her favorite color. (Make a gift certificate for it, if necessary, or ask her friends for tips on her size and favorite design.)

25   Make her lunch in the morning, and enclose a small gift (such as a tiny book of poetry, chocolates, earrings or perfume.)

Dating

It was the end of August, and Leisha was four months pregnant with their first child. She was turning twenty-seven on the 29th, but wasn't in the mood for celebrating. Hot weather, shorts that wouldn't fit anymore and wild mood swings didn't give her much reason to celebrate.

On her birthday morning, Larry offered to take her for a drive. Well, it would be a distraction at least, and the air conditioning would feel great—so they headed out. She adjusted the seat back and watched the scenery slide by. The town, the bridge, familiar exits—all were left behind. Where were they going?

By the time they reached the ferry terminal, Larry had handed her an envelope labeled #1. The coupon inside promised her a trip across the bay. They cuddled together on deck as the city came into view, and Leisha found envelope #2 slipped into her hands as the ferry docked. A seafood lunch on the waterfront!

The third was heavier than the rest—and decidedly green! It was filled with cash to go shopping and buy a beautiful maternity dress for Christmas. This was getting to be fun! How many more coupons were there? Each was decorated in hand-colored graphics; she was stunned that he had spent so much time preparing for her birthday.

In the sunshine and cool wind off the bay, they held hands as she looked for that dress. Coupon #4 brought them to a landmark, its 520-foot elevator ride and stunning view of the city. Out on this observation deck, she received the fifth envelope. Dinner! Yeah! They dined nearby at an international food festival, as she opened #6.

She just stared at the words inside the envelope—tickets to a jazz concert that would be starting in the next few minutes. She'd always wanted to hear this guy play live, but seats had been sold out for weeks! The seventh coupon was waiting as the concert ended—a chance to satisfy her craving for root beer floats (plural)! But envelope #8 was by far the best, the only coupon that didn't have an expiration date: a promise of romance that night—and forever.

Has your wife been on a date lately? Whether it lasts a couple of hours or an entire weekend, have a plan, invite her out and make it memorable. It's one way to ensure that love never expires!

J.C.

Blessings

26   Buy fabric paint at a craft or fabric store and design a T-shirt for her (a shirt that invites her on a weekend getaway).

27   Buy ice cream cones and head for a photo booth. (For under $2.00 you can get four crazy photos of the two of you crammed in front of the camera!)

28   Invite her out to a fancy "business" lunch.

29   Purchase a paperback Shakespeare, Miller, Williams or O'Neill, and hide tickets to the play inside!

30   Plan an all-day date. Start with muffins and coffee in bed, a walk in the park, and a visit to her favorite store (give her $20.00 to pick out a gift!). Purchase special lessons (golf, gourmet cooking, craft, etc.). Have a picnic with a view, bring a tape player or love poetry. Dine at her favorite restaurant and attend a local theater production or concert. And . . . .

Offering

Basketball! It was the regional play-off. One minute and thirty-five seconds left. The score was tied!

Time out.

The team consisted of two fifth-graders, three fourth-graders, one third-grader and a first-grader.

The first-grader—even though he was a real scrapper—had not yet played in the game. His father was the coach. He looked up into his father's eyes, and with eager anticipation, said, "Do you need me now, dad?"

He offered himself!

In the past, women have often been considered and treated by men as lesser beings. God is very clear in His Word that He didn't create inferior/superior beings. He did create us with different roles and different abilities! When God created marriage, He wasn't thinking on inferior/superior terms. Nor was God thinking "perfect." God was thinking, "together." Together has to do with need. And need has to do with respect.

You may not be a champion. You may not feel like a winner. You may not feel like you have anything to offer. But—you would be a champion to her if, when there's little time left and the score is tied, you look into her eyes and say, "Do you need me now, dear?"

That's offering yourself!

G.E.

Blessings

31 Offer your time. Before she asks, offer to take care of the kids so she can have some time alone.

32 Offer your talent. Before she asks, offer to help her complete a project—use your skills to enable her to get it done on time (or even *early*)!

33 Offer your money. Before she asks, offer to buy her a new outfit, pay for a baby-sitter so you can go on a date, buy a book she needs, make a car repair, or treat her to a mini-vacation.

34 Offer your support. Before she asks, offer to support her during a family crisis—pray with her and back her up in what she has to do or say. Offer to attend a crucial meeting with her, or wait with her during a doctor's appointment she's worried about. Give verbal support for her dreams!

35 Offer your heart. Before she asks, tell her you love her—that she fills your heart!

Admiring

Brad and Nancy had been married for nine years. They had been blessed with two robust boys. Sometimes Nancy wondered about the "blessed" part. She was always tired and Brad was always busy.

Tonight was one of those rare nights. It was a birthday party at their friends' house. Everybody was happy. That was, until "that woman" showed up. Nancy didn't even know her name, but she certainly knew she was present. So did all the men, including Brad! She was about twenty-one years old, beautiful and she had a marvelous figure. She wore a two-hundred-dollar dress which fit her like a thousand dollars. She bounced around the crowd, smiling, laughing and touching men on the arm. Nancy thought she was disgusting, especially when she was introduced to Brad. Nancy watched a broad smile spread across Brad's face at the moment of introduction. As she watched his eyes, she wondered if she should offer him a measuring tape.

Inside, she thought, "I'm just an old, tired, worn-out bag. I can't compete anymore. I'll never be that beautiful again. I just don't measure up!" Brad was no dummy. He felt Nancy's muscles tighten. He saw the look in her eye. He quickly led her to a quiet spot, put his hands on her waist and looked straight into her eyes. "Nancy, you always were and you always will be the most beautiful woman in the world. I wouldn't want you to be like that girl. I married you because I adore you. You delight me in ways no other woman ever could. God has equipped you to meet my needs perfectly—and you do!"

He pulled her close and whispered, "Besides, you look absolutely beautiful tonight. Let's blow this place early and go for a walk down by the lake. I'll hold you and love you and—Hey, I'm getting short of breath!" He kissed her on the nose and led a glowing wife back into the party.

She was admired. She was beautiful. He wanted to be alone with her and take her for a walk by the lake. And she still made him short of breath. She was OK.

Do you admire her, love her, need her, look into her eyes and hold her? Does she feel old, worn-out and tired, or does she glow?

The answer may be up to you!

G.E.

16

Blessings

36   Let her know that you find her fascinating!

37   Wink at her from across the room.

38   Touch her and tell her how much you admire and appreciate her body.

39   Tell her that you'd like a picture of her for your office—and pay to have one taken professionally.

40   Pray for ways to show your admiration for her. "Heavenly Father, according to 1 Corinthians 13:8 and 13, the love You created never fails. It is the greatest gift I can give to my wife. Help me to show _____ my love and admiration as You intended."

Laughing

It was the dead of winter in central Wisconsin. Holidays. Cold outside, but warm inside. Uncle Ted and my father-in-law, Pa, were telling childhood stories!

It was more than funny; it was hilarious! It really didn't matter if the story was humorous. Uncle Ted and Pa put on the funniest, most hilarious show ever. By the time they were halfway through their story, they were laughing so hard they were crying. We laughed with them until our sides hurt!

What precious moments. Those stories were windows into the past. Windows into joy. Windows into my wife's childhood. Windows into the heart of Uncle Ted and Pa. Hearts that could laugh and be silly! Hearts that could laugh at themselves!

At the age of thirty-five I changed my career. I left a building business and studied psychology and Bible. I'm afraid I left something else—my laugh! I guess I was deluded into thinking psychologists and preachers didn't laugh.

At our Christmas gathering a few years ago, my own children started telling stories—about me—and them! What a surprise I had. My children had pulled all kinds of fast ones on 'serious' old dad who didn't know how to laugh. A chuckle sprang up from deep within me, then an open laugh followed by a real old-fashioned belly laugh. Soon I was wiping my eyes and holding my sides. My children had helped me find my laugh again! I joined in and gave them some "wisdom literature"—some of Uncle Ted and Pa's real "belly busters"!

Someone asked a particular person who was always laughing if he thought Jesus laughed all the time. "I don't know," he replied, "but Jesus sure fixed me so I can laugh!"

I wonder if Jesus has fixed you so you can laugh? Especially at yourself! A good "belly buster" might do wonders for you. I know one thing, your wife and kids will love it. Laughter provides precious moments!

G.I.

18

Blessings

41   Clip out a cartoon or joke and leave it on the bathroom mirror for everyone to enjoy.

42   For a real "veg out" night: bring home tacos, rent Three Amigos (with Chevy Chase, Martin Short and Steve Martin) and just hang out and laugh!

43   At the beginning of each year, pick up a daily calendar that sports a joke on each page. Set it near the breakfast table to start the day with laughter—or at least a smile!

44   Let your kids know you can laugh at yourself. Make ice cream sundaes and get ready to tell them about "your most embarrassing moment(s)!"

45   Remember three funny stories from childhood or high school. Record them on a cassette tape and play them for your wife or kids some evening. (Let them keep the tape.)

Teaching

When I was young, our family of five went camping a lot. We preserved the camper's "code of honor," and cooked over the fire, hiked in the woods, listened as forest rangers described how to survive on slugs for protein, and piled into a musty, cozy canvas tent at night. We were rain magnets!

When it didn't rain, we had the chance to explore. We collected treasures to bring home. Rocks, shells, interesting bark and dried flowers. One of those treasures still sits on my parents' mantle. It's been preserved all this time, and we've carried with us when we've moved. This tiny wooden bird is carved simply, but the memories it evokes are priceless.

I remember the afternoon when it was made. The three of us girls went wading. Where the river parted, there was a small island we just had to explore! Dad joined us, and soon he had picked up a soft piece of wood, smaller than his hand. We squatted in our rubber boots, watching him gently carve into it. He showed us how to hold the blade to keep from digging in too deep, and how to shave wood just a little at a time. We followed every movement. Slowly, a tiny beak appeared, a head, then the contours of a wing and tail. This wonderful bird was formed before our very eyes! For the finishing touch, dad helped us rub dandelion flowers into the grain, giving the bird a soft, golden glow.

Yup, our dad was amazing! I was thrilled to learn how to carve—to have this secret ability to tuck under my belt. I was thrilled that dad took the time to teach me.

Jesus also taught. He taught His disciples about God and what to do with what they knew. They were empowered. What can you teach your wife? What special ability would she love to have? Make time this week to invest in her and teach her something new. It can empower her, too!

J.C.

Blessings

46 Write a note to her today, and ask her if there is anything she'd like you to teach her. Follow up and set a date to do it! (Ask her to teach you something new as well.)

47 Teach her one of your favorite sports this weekend! Do everything you can to make sure equipment, time and location will contribute to her success.

48 Share a special interest with her. Give her tips on how to use the video camera; make your world-famous BBQ sauce; tie a fly for fishing; make stock investments; use a jigsaw and drill press; or fly a plane!

49 Teach her something crazy—to whistle through her fingers, make a perfect water balloon or tell an outrageous joke!

50 Teach her how to love you by setting an example. (How do you want to be loved? A special meal? Long, passionate kisses? A back rub? Her undivided attention? Great sex?) Be the first to bless her as you would like to be blessed.

Including

He bounced into the house at 5:30 PM, thinking about the softball game. Play-off time! Grab a sandwich and a drink, change clothes and hurry to the game!

"Honey, why are you sitting there at the table? We're in the play-offs tonight. Where is my sandwich? Where are the kids? What . . .What?" he said as he noticed her eyes. She had been crying! He quickly moved over and put his hand on her shoulder. "What is the matter, honey?"

Slowly she slid the checkbook out from under the yellow pad in front of her. "Honey, I just don't have enough money to pay this last bill! And I have tried, honestly I have and I still can't make it!" The tears started flowing again as she admitted this.

"Listen, dear. Come here and let me hold you for a minute. I know you are trying hard. I'm trying too. And it is going to be all right! I love you. If I had a million dollars I would trust you with it. " Pause. "Well, maybe I would check the balance once a week or so!" he teased with a slight grin. "Now, let's freshen up, grab a sandwich and go yell our insides out at the game. We will talk about this later tonight when it's calm and quiet."

Later that evening they asked each other what their number-one purpose was in life. They planned and determined goals for the next three years, the next year and the next month. Now they both had something to commit to. Both of them were included. They knew where they were going to be when they got where they were going.

Does your wife know where your life is going? Is she included in the plan? Does she know it? Maybe you should put your hand on her shoulder and say, "Honey, it's going to be all right. I have a plan. Let's talk about it tonight, in calm and quiet!"

G.J.

Blessings

51   Include her in your job. Describe a project you've been working on, or share a company brochure, catalog, or video related to your work.

52   Ask her to help you learn how to cook your favorite meal.

53   Buy a book on something you're both interested in (camping, music, improving your sex life, travel, art, investment, etc.). Read aloud to each other before bed.

54   Sign up for a community education class together. Include each other in something you would like to learn (golf, woodworking, auto repair, dancing, etc.).

55   Plan a "how-to" video night. (Public libraries are a great resource!) After the kids are asleep, watch and learn how to include her in your "expertise" (remodeling, gourmet cooking, landscaping, etc.).

Surprising

As the recovery room doors swung shut behind her, she felt a cool breeze from the hallway brush over her cheeks and hair. It felt so good to be out! An I.V. dangled from her left arm, and she felt the tug of it against her wrist as she was wheeled forward. Lots of lights. Flashes of lights, and that soft, warm, muggy feeling that lingers after sedatives. She wiggled her fingers and toes. Everything worked—but sluggishly. Then her fingers pressed at the bandages around her throat. It almost didn't feel like her neck was under there anywhere. Just numbness.

By the time the morning shift arrived, she was stirring underneath a pile of cotton blankets. Someone else was in the room, and watching her. It was Steve! She touched the ring she had given him on their fifteenth wedding anniversary as he fumbled to hold both her hands. "They didn't find anything! Those lumps in your throat were benign!" he exclaimed. Relief flooded her. It washed away all the knots in her stomach. All the pressing fear she had been battling for weeks now. It was over. She was clean!

At first, resting at home was easy—she didn't feel like doing much at all. But she felt odd, like she'd been given a second chance and shouldn't waste even one moment. Friends kept coming to mind, people she hadn't seen for years. "I want to get back into life again, Steve," she explained. "The kids are gone and busy, and I want to be out there too, seeing people and enjoying myself."

One morning three weeks after her surgery, she discovered an envelope taped to her clock radio. As she opened the note inside, a plane ticket slipped out. Steve had carefully lettered "SURPRISE!" at the top of the page. "Enclosed you will find the ticket to 'get out there, see people and enjoy yourself!' Destination: Boulder, Colorado. HAVE FUN! Love, Steve."

A complete surprise! A whole week to visit Laurie, her closest friend from school. She ran to the kitchen where Steve was making coffee and hugged him hard. "It's perfect," she cried. "It's exactly what I needed!"

What exactly does your wife need? A weekend alone? A special gift? A romantic getaway with you? Take some time this month and plan to surprise her!

J.C.

Blessings

56   Buy her a cassette or CD of her favorite music. Surprise her by hiding it in the glove compartment in her car.

57   Surprise her with a sign that says, "I love you," hidden in her flower garden.

58   Pick up some special deli food, and invite her favorite friends over for a surprise "carpet picnic." (Take the kids to play miniature golf or to watch a movie.)

59   Surprise her with a plane ticket to visit friends or relatives.

60   Copy some love poetry or write a bit of your own. (For romance in unexpected places, tape it to the inside of a kitchen cupboard or the front of a window shade.)

Parenting

Current research shows there are few things in the world more important than parenting. Children are born into this world like sponges. Each child is waiting to soak up love, nurture, affirmation, encouragement and hope. The development of the brain is influenced by good parenting.

In the face of these facts, mothers and fathers stream into counselors because of "time poverty." Not enough time! Both mom and dad are working in full-time jobs. Mom often pulls double duty in two full-time jobs—one in the market place and one at home.

Consider Sara: She gets up at 5:00 AM. She has a twenty-minute quiet time, showers, makes the kids lunches, wakes the kids and drives to work, putting on her make-up as she drives. Sara's husband, Mike, gets the kids on the bus. Sara is back home at 4:00 to chauffeur the kids to school functions, help with homework, cook supper, do the dishes and get the kids ready for bed. Mike arrives home at 9:30 PM. By then, Sara is exhausted.

Of course, there is still the cleaning and laundry. Sometimes Sara wishes she could run away and not come back.

Without two parents planning properly to share the load, every mom can be in Sara's situation!

How important is your wife? Your children? Do adequate hugs and kisses and affirmation and encouragement and hope really influence the development of your child's brain? Are you spending adequate time planning and helping your wife parent? What if you are wrong?!

G.I.

Blessings

61   Each month, put aside a block of 2-3 hours to be alone with each child.

62   Talk to other parents who are struggling with "time poverty." (Are there any who aren't?) Set up house-cleaning, baby-sitting or yard work co-ops. Together, hire students from your church who will set a reasonable fee if you provide them with regular work opportunities. Use that extra time as family time!

63   Pick one Saturday each month that is off limits to friends or other relatives. Let the kids know they have input in the day's activities. (See an air show, take a hike, visit a water park, or learn a sport together!)

64   Drop a treat or a short note into your kids' lunches every once in a while. (Let them know you think about them during the day.)

65   Tell them about another father—their Heavenly Father. Help them become comfortable praying to Him and excited about reading His Word!

Assisting

In our kitchen sits an old wooden stool. The paint is milky-thick and it is peeling in places. One rung is especially worn, where a foot has rested over and over again. Each time I see that rung, I remember the man whose dark-brown work shoe left its mark so indelibly.

The stool sat in another kitchen nearly sixty years, at the end of the counter, right next to the flour bin. In my mind, I can smell the clean, warm scent of soap suds, see the bow on my grandmother's apron tied carefully in back. I can hear her rhythmic voice while she scrubbed, rinsed and stacked—hear the clink of dishes being washed in a porcelain sink.

And there is the heel of a brown work shoe hooked firmly over the stool rung. My grandfather's work shoe. It was my job to find "homes" for each dish and utensil, carefully putting them away. But grandfather dried them—vigorously—with a soft, old towel. He seemed a giant of a man to me. Big, imposing, and sometimes gruff.

His hands were fascinating. They weren't soft or graceful like my doctor's hands, they were massive and roughly scarred from work. They didn't bend smoothly or hold small objects easily. I could picture him playing football in high school, playing pranks on my grandmother's younger sister, and riding his wild motorcycle in the '20s. But drying dishes? That's what struck me. He overwhelmed the kitchen and this frail stool, yet here he was, handling delicate china.

I sense this was an important ritual for him, a role he was content to play out of love for my grandmother. It was here in the evening that they would work and talk, a time he could assist her in some small way.

Choose one task this week with which you can assist your wife. Decide to make it meaningful! This time together may become a legacy of blessing to her—and the next generations as well!

J.C.

Blessings

66   Pray for insight. "Heavenly Father, according to Galatians 6:9-10, you warn me not to become tired of doing good to your children. You promise to show me special opportunities to assist my wife. If I don't give up, you promise to bless both of us. Thank you."

67   Create a book of coupons for her. (Offer your assistance to help her do her least favorite chores!)

68   Volunteer at least once a day. Make a point to assist her with a task before she asks! (Work together on dishes, errands, children's homework, meals, laundry, etc.)

69   Assist with her job, classwork, or home projects. (Kindly critique her performance as she practices a seminar presentation. Quiz her before a big test. Design a play structure for the children together.)

70   List all the weekly chores on small slips of paper. Place in a bowl and draw out an equal number of slips between you. Your assistance may cut her work week in half.

Remembering

It was her birthday! Would he remember? Would he think of some special gift? Maybe it would be roses! She loved roses, especially yellow roses!

He did remember! With a big grin he presented her with twelve red roses. There was a big problem! They were artificial. They were dead! She couldn't hide the negative emotions flying around in her mind like stones in an old tin can.

"But I thought . . . ." He could see it was no use.

"Even though these roses are beautiful and would remind me again and again of your love, I am still disappointed. I don't want artificial roses—even once. It would mean so much if you would just give me one living yellow rose. Yellow roses stand for hope. My greatest hope is that you enjoy living with me!"

Her parents had great hope when she was born. She read in her baby book that her father had brought a yellow rose to the hospital when she was born. When she was twelve her grandfather gave her a yellow rose at her baptism. It was a symbol of the hope of eternal life!

What a smart husband—he quickly returned the sixty-four dollar artificials, bought six yellow roses, and saved fifty-two dollars! What a smart wife—she shared her innermost feelings and needs. What a great birthday. A birthday filled with hope. A birthday *and a lesson* to remember!

G.I.

Blessings

71   Remember special dates. (If necessary, keep a list of them in your wallet. At the first of each year, add them to your office or personal calendar.)

72   Help her remember a special trip or a visit to an outstanding museum. (Buy her a small memento—a postcard to frame, a scarf, a framed print, an ornament, etc.)

73   Remember her favorite gifts. (Keep a list of those she really enjoyed receiving.)

74   Remember her sizes and favorite colors. Ask her to write them down for you, and keep them in your wallet for spontaneous gift giving!

75   Remember to plan ahead. Whenever a birthday or anniversary is approaching, leave a reminder on your calendar one or two weeks in advance. (If she has experienced a loss—such as a parent or child—make a note of that date and be sensitive to her mood as that day approaches next year.)

Planning

All she wanted was five acres with a creek running through it. A place where the kids could run and yell and play with abandon. A safe place. A good place.

All he wanted was another rental property. A good structure. A good location. A good investment.

She was dreaming of the future—the future of her children. Dreaming of healthy memories of enjoying God in nature, memories of enjoying God in family, memories of building something from nothing, memories of praying around a fire as the wind whispered through the pines. Together. Peace.

He was dreaming of the future too. Christian education. Tuition. Cars. Insurance. Providing financial resources for his children that he never had. Security!

What was wrong with their thinking? Nothing. Except they treated each other's thinking as controversial. They needed to recognize and value each other's dreams.

They were twenty-eight years old. In fourteen years their children would be in college. They would only be forty-two years old. Lots of time for financial investment. However, if they didn't share in their children's lives now, it would soon be too late. Her dreams were crucial *now!*

Children are like books. Every day you write on the pages of their future. Your dreams acted out in reality are being recorded on the pages of your child's future!

Plan together. Write healthy memories for your children. Ask Holy Spirit to help. Then dream again!

G.E.

Blessings

76   Share the individual dreams you have for one year, five years and ten years. Record these in a small book and refer to them often!

77   Agree to pray for one month about these dreams for yourself and for her. Pray for wisdom according to James 1:5.

78   Make a date to discuss and prioritize these dreams. (The conclusions you reach should bring peace to *both* of you—not anxiety!)

79   Set up a long-term calendar to record the time frame you plan for the realization of each dream. (Have a quarterly "board meeting" to be certain that goals are being met and that you are still dreaming *together!*)

80   Encourage her to have short-term dreams as well. On the first day of each month, ask her to tell you her "number one" dream. (See what you can do to make it come true!)

Celebrating

It was their tenth anniversary. He had thought about it for months. This was his invitation: "Honey, I'll get a baby-sitter. I want to take you out to celebrate!"

"What?" she exclaimed! "What? What!"

"Just wait and see!" he said with a grin.

When she awoke on their anniversary day, he presented her with a card. He gave her a red rose. The kids served her breakfast in bed. At noon, he called and wished her "happy anniversary" and told her he loved her.

At 5:00 PM, he appeared at the door looking like a million dollars. As he kissed her, he held a corsage hidden behind his back. Her favorite color! Next came a quiet boat ride. He stopped in a secluded cove—the very place he had proposed to her ten years ago! Suddenly, a man in a wet suit surfaced near the side of the boat with a bottle of sparkling cider and two goblets on a silver tray. They toasted each other. He proposed again, and she said, "Oh, yes!" just like she did the first time.

After docking, they took off on a peaceful little drive. He stopped at an overlook where they had walked on their first date. Two friends appeared, set up a table for two, and served them salads. On to the home of other friends for the entree. In a moment, a violinist appeared and played music they enjoyed while dating.

She couldn't help wondering what else was in store for them tonight. So far, at each stop, she was greeted by close friends—she couldn't wait for dessert! He took her for a midnight drive into the mountains, stopping for her favorite hot fudge sundaes. Then on to a secluded, mountain cabin and a canopy bed with small, twinkling lights overhead.

Just before they went to sleep, he slipped an anniversary diamond on her finger and whispered, "Thanks for ten wonderful years. I love you more today. I'll love you more tomorrow!"

With a little planning, this husband could be you!

G.E.

Blessings

81   Pray for a spirit of celebration. "Heavenly Father, according to Proverbs 19:14, my wife is a gift from You. According to Proverbs 5:18, I can receive Your blessings—rejoicing and celebrating in her!"

82   Celebrate her new job or promotion. Buy a congratulations card, and make it into a coupon redeemable for one professional outfit. Shop for it together and take her out for dessert afterward!

83   Remember the best date you ever had together? Celebrate by recreating it as much as possible. Tell her why you're still falling in love with her!

84   Celebrate her success. Has she just pitched a no-hitter for her softball team? Received an "A" in her night class? Lost ten pounds? Help the kids make a poster to let her know you've all noticed!

85   Make her birthday memorable. (Consider her wishes: a big party, a few friends, or just you and her?) Plan a creative celebration! Surprise her over at a friend's home—where everyone has chipped in to buy her something *really* special. Or let her choose an all-day adventure—for just the two of you!

Writing

I'm staying inside this morning. The sky is a deep, dead gray—lowered over our city like a giant lid. Even wind doesn't seem to interrupt the steady drizzle. Wrapped in quilts and leaning against our old maple dresser, I'm sorting through a box of letters. I've counted over fifty of them—heavy linen envelopes inscribed with delicate black ink, a letter to him, followed by one from her. Their first correspondence is an invitation: Would she like to attend a football game with him? Her reply, carefully copied onto a clean page, graciously accepts.

Months later, he is working long hours at his father's business. She is away at school.

SHE: "This may be awful foolish but I feel so terribly lonesome for the sight of just one man, and long just to talk to him even if I did just send a letter to him only yesterday . . . ."

HE: "My how glad I am to get letters from you. When you get home I am going to give you the biggest hug you have ever had in your life. I get so lonesome that I have to go and read your letters over again, because then it seems as if you were closer . . . ."

SHE: "I'd give anything to be home tonight . . . . I've seen you so many times in my mind today—just imagining so much, that the reality would be blissful . . . ."

HE: "Sunday night and hungry for the sight of a certain brown eyed girl, honestly this summer seems to lengthen out instead of growing shorter . . .I may sound pessimistic, but there isn't a thing that has any attraction to me as long as you're not here to share it."

The letters, dated over seventy years ago, continue for months. Not one seems to be missing from the box. A lasting record of love preserved through all these years—for their children—and for me, one of their grandchildren.

It is a rare tenderness when thoughts are preserved in writing. When you're away from your wife, think about what you miss most—and write it down. It doesn't take expensive cards or fancy stationery to give her a lasting record of your love.

J.C.

Blessings

86   Send her a postcard—just because.

87   After an argument, write a letter to talk about the problem. (Describe what is still difficult for you to understand and what you hope to heal.) Ask to meet her somewhere away from home where you can discuss the matter again.

88   Write love notes: "I love you because . . . ." Hide them in her closet, dresser drawers, the pocket of her robe, purse, etc.

89   Create a "written portrait." Study her as she works, reads, walks, talks to the children or listens to music. What do you see? What do you like most? What haven't you noticed before? (Write these observations on colored paper and enclose them in an inexpensive frame. She'll love this "fine art!")

90   Send a delayed message. When you've had a great day together, write her a note to tell her how much you enjoyed being with her and why. Seal it in an envelope. Next time there are difficulties between you, mail the letter to her as a reminder of your love.

Honoring

"For Hopedale High School, at five-foot-eight, captain and right guard, Glenn Egli-i-i-i!" I think it was the first time I had ever heard my name announced in public. I'm sure it was the first time that anyone applauded when my name was mentioned. I was thrilled!

A name. How important is it? In many cultures, a name is everything. Why? Because a name describes character. The name "Linda" means "beautiful." "Barnabas" means "encouragement" or "encourager." "Paul" means "little." "Asher" means "joy." "Megan" means "mighty" or "strength."

Perhaps you have never considered the meaning of your name. You may not even like your name because you associate it with something or someone you don't care for. But I know this: Whatever your name is, it is something personal. It is you. And whenever you hear your name, something is triggered—something personal and special.

To say someone's name is to say something special. It is to directly address character, or the spirit which creates character. To address someone by their personal name is to honor them, to touch them in a special way. To address someone by their personal name is to remove distance between you. Try it. Look into her eyes. And, in a loving way, simply say her name. In your spirit and with your actions, honor her character. She'll be thrilled!

G.E.

Blessings

91   Plant a tree or rosebush to honor her. Commemorate a goal she's reached, a special accomplishment or promotion. (It may be a symbol of honor to her for a lifetime!)

92   Address her by name. Instead of saying, "honey," "dear," "hey, you" (or worse), honor her by using her name when getting her attention or getting involved in a discussion!

93   Honor her in public. Introduce her by name and with pride to friends and colleagues. Let them know she is well worth meeting!

94   Honor her family and friends. Use their proper names. Speak of them with respect, out of love for her!

95   "Heavenly Father, according to 1 Peter 3:7, help me to honor _____. Help me to be considerate of her, to appreciate her special qualities, to treat her with respect, and to see her as a partner with me in the gracious gift of life, so that nothing will hinder my prayers to You."

Serving

The gospels give us glimpses of Jesus' ministry, what He said, who was healed, where He went, and what difficulties He encountered. In effect, they let us walk with Jesus. Though some accounts are more detailed than others, one characteristic stands out—Jesus' compassion and heartfelt desire to serve others. From people who needed physical healing, to those with deep emotional hurts, demon torment or hunger, He used His God-given gifts to serve and meet those needs.

When we glimpse Jesus with His closest friends at Passover, we see a poignant portrayal of service. He had a master plan for the Last Supper. He chose a special location in a quiet, upstairs room. He made arrangements for food, giving His disciples specific instructions for that day. He tells them in Luke 22, *I have eagerly desired to eat this Passover with you before I suffer.*

As God's only Son, Jesus could have expected that these arrangements be made for Him. He could have expected to be taken care of and served. Instead, He shows his love for them by washing their feet, praying over them, and offering them the bread and wine of a new covenant. It is His service, His sacrifice and His blood that seal the covenant.

Imagine how the disciples must have felt just before the Passover— they had traveled miles on foot, gone without food and been constantly hounded by the controversy surrounding their Teacher. They must have felt physically spent and emotionally drained—yet Jesus chose the simple act of serving a meal to meet both needs.

Perhaps a new covenant needs to be made between you and your wife. What simple acts of service could meet her needs? First John 3:18 teaches us to love not only with the words we speak, but also with our actions . . . .

J.C.

Blessings

96   Wake up early to help her get ready for a morning appointment. (Serve her breakfast and pack a special lunch!)

97   Wash and clean her car—just because!

98   Gently brush her hair after she's experienced a stressful day.

99   Cook an international meal for her, and say "I love you" in each language represented. (The library is a great resource!)

100   Read her favorite book aloud while she bathes and relaxes in the tub.

Decision-Making

How do a husband and wife make decisions?

At a retreat for young women several years ago, a wise speaker tackled this question. The inevitable subject of "submission" came up, and most of us waited with bristling hair on the backs of our necks to hear such advice as: Never discuss an issue without being asked. Obey your husband's decisions. Don't interfere. Don't question. Don't participate, etc. Well, she surprised all of us!

She described significant events in her nearly forty-year marriage. It was obvious how much she loved her husband. I don't remember if she used those words, but affection showed in her eyes whenever she spoke of him. As they made decisions over the years, they became partners. She spoke firmly against what she called "guerrilla tactics" when decisions are made. "If your husband doesn't include you in decision making," she said, "don't withhold information from him and wait for him to make a mistake, fall on his face, and be greeted with 'I told you so.' Rather, we are called as wives to give wise consideration and open input into each decision."

At the close of our retreat, she encouraged us to bless our husbands. Her parting words challenged our energy, intelligence, experience and prayer life to help make Godly decisions with our husbands.

A marriage partnership requires that the opinions of both people be considered when a decision is made. Proverbs 31 describes this marriage partnership and a woman of noble character—*She speaks with wisdom, and faithful instruction is on her tongue* (v.26). *Her husband has full confidence in her and lacks nothing of value*(v.11).

Next time an important decision needs to be made, give your wife the opportunity to become a Proverbs 31 woman. Incorporate truth, togetherness and time. Pray for God's truth to be revealed. Ask your wife's opinion, considering the pros and cons together. Take time to discuss options and make the best decision.

J.C.

Blessings

101   Pray for God's truth and wisdom as you begin to make a decision together.

102   Treat her as an equal. Spend as much time considering her opinions as you do your own.

103   Meet her halfway. If her understanding would be aided by a thorough look at facts or a visual chart/graph, willingly offer that information.

104   Follow through on your decisions. Make it possible for her to count on you and trust you.

105   Admit mistakes and alter decisions accordingly. (If no common ground can be found, be willing to accept a friend or expert as mediator.)

Dreaming

He came bursting into the house with that over-grown teenager look! She recognized it immediately. He was up to something. There was a twinkle in his eye and a spring in his step. He put his hands on her hips, kissed her on the end of her nose, and said, "Know what!?"

"No", she replied, "but I have a feeling I will soon!"

Like a tumbling mountain stream, words cascaded from within him. "Honey, that dream house, that property with a view I've always wanted, I found it! It needs some fixing later, but we can afford it!"

Outside she smiled, but inside she grimaced. "What about my dream?" she thought. A cute, decorated, finished house is my dream! I have lived in this house for six years and it isn't finished!

She decided to risk. "Honey, I love your dream. I'd like to see this dream property, but first, can I share my dream with you?"

He kept his hands on her hips, but he backed up several inches. "Suu—suuuu—sure!" he stammered.

"Honey, if we buy this property, I'd like to borrow enough money to finish it now, to decorate, to make it cute. I'm not sure why, but that is very important to me. In fact, it would make me feel important if you would do that for me." Then, almost as if it was too painful to share, she said quietly, "My dream has been on hold for soooooo long!"

"Why, honey, I guess—I, well—" He just stood there for a minute as if speechless. "Uhhhhh, honey, I guess I have been pretty dense concerning your dream. Help me understand more."

She wiggled loose from his arms, grabbed his hand and said, "Later. Let's go look at our dream!"

G.E.

Blessings

106 Let her know that dreaming is OK and even encouraged. Tell her it would give you joy to make her dreams come true!

107 Make each wedding anniversary a time to discuss your dreams. Make sure you can understand her dreams. (Describe them to her in your own words.)

108 Is she dreaming about having a beautiful garden, or a wardrobe? Buy a book to help her envision the dream!

109 Need financial help to make a dream reality? Meet with a volunteer financial advisor at church or in your community. (Public libraries and banks can often refer you to such individuals.)

110 If possible, find a print or card that illustrates her dream. (Buy an inexpensive frame and hang it where it will remind you both to dream and pray about it.)

Helping

Two favorite pictures in my baby album are photos of my parents. These tiny images are more than scenes, they are snapshots of their marriage. Shortly before I was born, a picture shows mom grinning from atop their cottage roof where she's helping dad shingle. The other, taken just after I was born, shows dad giving me a bath, chuckling because my head is fashionably decorated with a washcloth.

I know now what that year was like for them—it was filled with the uncertainty of newlyweds, financial stresses and a work schedule that often kept dad away from early morning to late evening. They needed each other, they needed encouragement and they needed help. Despite what elements were at work outside their marriage, inside they were committed to help each other—regardless of what seemed easiest or most comfortable.

As a young girl, I remember being impressed by those photos. As I grew older, I learned that they lived what they taught. There wasn't a double standard in their marriage. They shared responsibilities. It didn't matter if the job was difficult or boring or "beneath" them. When we three girls needed school clothes, dad took us. And he didn't grump around and complain about it. He made it into an adventure! Each one of us was treated to a day alone with him, breakfast at a restaurant and shopping at the spot of our choice—sometimes in a nearby town.

When our garage needed to be completed in a hurry, mom was out there helping dad steady beams and raise rafters. The other person's project was a priority. They made help available to each other.

In what ways can you share your wife's responsibilities? How can you offer to help lighten her workload this week? Galatians 6:2 calls for us to help share each other's burdens—not as a suggestion or a possibility, but as a way of fulfilling the law of Christ!

J.C.

Blessings

111   Allow her to make a list of projects, and help her finish them!

112   During a busy week, fill up the gas tank of her car.

113   Help friends and family members when they need it. (She doesn't need to be the only caregiver!)

114   Be approachable. Respond with kind words and willing actions. If she needs help, make it easy for her to ask—anytime.

115   "Heavenly Father, help me to want to help my wife. In Hebrews 4:16, You promise that I can approach You with confidence, receiving Your forgiveness and compassion to help me whenever I need it. I want my wife to be able to approach me in the same way!"

Scheduling

During my years in the business world I found scheduling to be very important and rewarding. I could tell you with fair accuracy what I would be doing three weeks from next Monday. As I studied for the ministry, I planned to run my pastorate in the same manner. It did not work. In the business world, I could use force. I could fire people if they did not do what I directed. Force and manipulation do not work in the pastorate nor in the Christian family. God's character *does* work.

God's character does not tell people what to do. God's character leads. Force and leadership are two completely different processes. As God's character began to flow through me, my congregation began to follow. My schedules were altered again and again. I did not stop scheduling. I just started to consult and include Holy Spirit in my scheduling.

I prayed as if everything depended on God. I scheduled and worked as if everything depended on me. It was a great combination. Now I was not just scheduling and working, I was participating in empowered working!

Including God's Holy Spirit in my scheduling did not come easy. For a time, I considered stopping scheduling all together. But when I did, everything drifted into chaos. Stopping scheduling was a serious mistake. God did not want me to stop scheduling. He just wanted to be the Divine Choreographer of my scheduling.

What does this have to do with my wife? Everything! Wives need the security and direction of a husband who schedules. Like Holy Spirit, they need to be included in the planning and scheduling. After all, Holy Spirit lives within wives!

When you include your wife in your scheduling you include Holy Spirit. What is the effect? She will have great calm, and peace in her spirit. She will have great confidence in you. And she will be willing to allow Holy Spirit to work through her to make your common schedule work.

Holy Spirit and your wife are great partners in scheduling. Include your wife. She and God will love it!

G.E.

48

Blessings

116 Buy a wall-sized calendar for the kitchen and schedule events *with* your wife and children.

117 Ask the whole family to meet for "munchies" on Sunday evenings. Take a half hour together to schedule the week in advance!

118 Schedule a date with her. Mark it on the calendar, but surprise her with "what" and "where"!

119 Schedule work and family events carefully. Set a good example—when things don't go as planned—call if you'll be late!

120 Schedule "breaks" or rest periods. Make sure there are days on the calendar that are empty and "off limits" for any outside activities.

Protecting

She wasn't thin, trim or fit. She was skinny. Her color was pasty. Dark rings shadowed her dull, yet angry eyes. Her nervous movements signaled insecurity and anxiety. She lived in fear—fear that she was condemned. A pervasive influence in this world had affected her directly and personally. This influence took on the disguise of another person, but it was not. The direct and personal influence was Satan and his demons.

C.S. Lewis warned us regarding Satan and demons: Don't disbelieve in their existence; and don't have an excessive and unhealthy interest in them.

Are the words of the Apostle Paul relevant? *For our struggle is not against flesh and blood, but against the rulers, against the authorities, against the powers of this dark world and against the spiritual forces of evil in the heavenly realms* (Eph. 6:12).

Satan's schemes had left this woman with bitterness, cynicism, anger, envy, insecurity and an inconsistent prayer life. Inside and outside she was crying when she needed to be fighting. It wasn't that she couldn't resist. She just didn't have the strength to do battle. She was asking for help!

What help did she need? She needed a husband who knew he was a man of God. A husband who knew that it was his God-given role to protect his wife and children from Satan and demons by prayer. A husband who prayed aloud. A husband who prayed while holding her in his arms. Sheltering. Protecting.

Today, her countenance is brighter. Her eyes are beginning to shine. Her spirit is learning to sing again—slowly. How? She asked, and her husband responded by fulfilling his role as a man of God. As protector. Just in time! Are you filling your role as man of God?

G.E.

Blessings

121 Help her feel safe. Make sure all outside doors lock properly, the porch lights work and the house is secure while you're away.

122 When something or someone has frightened her, resist the impulse to tease. Put your arms around her and hold her!

123 Protect her in public. Let her and everyone else know that she is in your care and safe with you. Don't allow others to threaten her—even when it may be a joke that's been taken too far.

124 Seriously consider her fears. Legitimize her feelings of fright or dread by listening, praying and taking steps to combat what causes them.

125 Pray over her and the children before bed. Let them know that God is protecting them through your prayers. "Heavenly Father, according to Matthew 18:18-19, Satan and evil are bound on behalf of this family, and I loose Your angels to protect them as they sleep."

Ministering

I opened the door to our lobby. In the corner of my eye, I saw her. She was sitting on the front edge of a chair. Her posture told me she was in pain. My insides seemed to twist and knot as I realized it was my wife.

"I hurt my back," she said. She sat quietly, just looking into my eyes. Was it shame I saw there? Failure? Internally I prayed that it was neither. Did she feel sad knowing it was my birthday? Was she thinking this might ruin our birthday 'date'?

From within, I heard a voice saying, "Help her, dummy!"

As she walked slowly into my office, I prepared a firm chair for her to sit on. I gently began to rub her tight muscles as I prayed prayers based on Scriptures.

She began to relax as I prayed, professing healing into her body. She spoke softly—"I feel better already, just having you touch me."

I wonder what kind of pain your wife could be experiencing today? Minister to her. Touch her and pray. Perhaps she will say, "I feel better already—!"

G.F.

Blessings

126 Give her time and a place to recover. She may not feel like she has time to rest! Fill the tub with warm water, bath salts, and let her know she won't be interrupted.

127 Before an important doctor's appointment, find comics, a humorous book or stories to take her mind off worries in the waiting room.

128 Give her a soothing massage. Rub her forehead, temples, shoulders, back, legs and feet. Gently.

129 Take her mind off pain. When she's ill in bed, visit the library and bring back special books and video tapes for her!

130 Pray for healing: "Heavenly Father, according to Matthew 8:15, Jesus died for our sins and our infirmities; and according to 1 Peter 2:24, *By the stripes of Jesus,* we can experience healing. In the name (character) of Jesus, be healed. Father, bring about this healing for _____ in a way that will please and bring honor to You."

Modeling

What an incredibly busy day. Rush here. Rush there. Hurry, hurry, hurry. She was nearly home from delivering the kids to baseball practice when she saw it. A billfold was laying on the side of the road. She quickly stopped and picked it up. To her surprise it contained $265! "Wow!" She thought. "What I could do with $265!"

She looked through the identification cards. It belonged to a man who lived two blocks away, in a fancy, expensive house with a yard that looked manicured. Something or someone whispered in her ear, "He will never miss it!" What should she do? Thoughts raced through her mind like the Indy 500. Maybe I should just take the money and drop the billfold off in his driveway. He doesn't need the money; he needs the billfold and the identification. He should be glad to get that! Or maybe I should just keep a hundred dollars for going to all this trouble. He'll never know what happened to it.

Then Rod came home. "Guess what I found today?" Rod looked through the billfold and said, "Let's go for a walk!"

"Where to?" She asked.

"Where else? To return this billfold and the money! That's what Christ would do."

All the questions rolling around like the Indy 500 ceased. She slid her arm under his and said, "Let's go! I'm so glad I am married to a man like you, an honest man, a man who models God's character."

G.F.

Blessings

131 Use Jesus' example to refine yourself and model His character before your wife and your children. (Strive to be her "knight in shining armor." Do you need to work on fitness? Controlling anger? Time spent in prayer? Finishing projects? Hygiene? Showing kindness?)

132 Pray for a clean start. "Heavenly Father, according to Psalm 51:10, I ask You to create in me a pure heart, and renew a steadfast and righteous spirit within me. I thank You for hearing and responding."

133 Guard your character more than property. Be quiet enough for Holy Spirit to use an "alarm system" in your spirit to alert you when you've slipped.

134 "Heavenly Father, according to 2 Peter 1:4, in Christ I can partake in Your divine nature. Through Jesus, it is flowing through my life as I rest in Him."

135 Being a "model" husband or father can bring a great deal of pressure—if you attempt to do it on your own. Fail alone, or succeed with God!

Listening

She was obviously nervous. She was wringing her hands. She kept glancing toward the door. "My husband didn't want me to come. He doesn't believe we need help. He says if I would just submit to him and do what he says, our problems would be over—maybe he is right!" She seemed exhausted, unable to go on.

"Tell me about your husband," I asked. "Why did you marry him?"

"Oh," she exclaimed. "He really seemed like a man of God. He never swore. He didn't drink alcohol. He didn't smoke. He went to church every Sunday. He went to every church clean-up day. He looked like 'Mr. Good Guy.' That was what I saw before we got married."

She leaned her head on her hand. "'Mr. Good Guy' turned into 'Mr. Big Boss'! He won't let me think for myself. I can't go anywhere without his approval. And he won't approve anything that is fun, just for me. I can't talk to any of my old friends at church because he is insanely jealous. He says a woman is to submit to her husband. That means to be seen and not heard. My opinion is worth absolutely nothing. Everybody seems to think he is such a fine Christian man. I think he is an impossible dictator. Maybe he is sick—in the head! What do you think?"

And what do you think? Is he a man of God? He is a man who is called Christian, but he is not a man of God! Men of God treat their wives with honor, with respect. Men of God are "servant leaders," not "big bosses."

A "servant leader" serves! He serves by modeling spiritual interest and practice, by ministering God's character to his wife and children. He serves by being unselfish, by leading toward common goals. He serves by encouraging his wife to excel in her areas of strength and by allotting specific time for his wife and children. He serves by seeing himself, his wife, and their children as an equal unit which he is responsible for. His first responsibility is to respond to God's ability. His second responsibility is to bless with God's ability. It is God's ability, but the initiative is his. He cannot accomplish either without listening both to God and to his wife!

G.E.

56

Blessings

136 Spend time in prayer each day, listening. God can then speak directly to you through words in the Bible, a clear thought during the day, or through people with whom you come in contact.

137 Watch for "misplaced distress." Does your wife seem anxious or panicked about a seemingly small detail? Listen to her—and see if you can't hear what is truly causing hurt.

138 Be attentive to your children. If they are speaking to you, listen. They might have a message that—later—you'll wish you had heard!

139 Listen to music together. (Don't try and talk or plan or discuss an issue.) Just listen.

140 Ask what is important to her—don't assume. Listen, and then repeat back what you believe she has said.

Leading

It came like a traffic accident. No warning. She looked across the table and spoke in a very deliberate manner. "I've thought it through from every possible angle. There is nothing else to think about. I'm leaving him." Why was I surprised? She didn't appear to be in depression. Oh, she looked a bit stressed, but who doesn't now and then? Trying to regain my composure, I simply asked her what brought her to such a monumental decision.

"I am in despair!" she said. "I am desperate. I thought I married a man of God, but I found out he is a passive wimp. He won't lead. He won't plan. He doesn't want to go to church. He has no goals. All he does is vegetate in front of that boob tube! He is just a nothing! I can't stand it anymore. I have two children, but I am raising three. He is just like another child. We have a one-parent family, and I am it! She stopped to breathe, but she hadn't stopped thinking. "I want to love him, but there is nothing to love. He is just becoming a big nothing. What am I supposed to do?"

I have met hundreds of wives like this woman. There are thousands—hundreds of thousands. And what should I tell her? Are you a nothing? A passive wimp? Are you vegging out in front of the television to escape your God-given obligation to lead? I think I can hear your reply: "And exactly how do I do that?" One thing is sure. We lead by what we are before we lead by what we say and do.

Why was Jesus an effective leader? Because He was the Presence of God happening. He was the Presence of God before He spoke and before He did anything. Jesus was the presence of supernatural righteousness happening. It was determining the course of His life. It gave Him destiny and purpose. He was a Man with a plan. Therefore, you could follow Him.

Husbands, unless you are actively exercising faith, praying and participating in God's righteousness, it is quite possible you may have no course for your life. You may be in drift. Soon, your wife may call you a passive wimp. And she will be right. Despair is soon to follow.

Pray. Participate and release supernatural righteousness in and through yourself. God will direct your life. Become a leader!

G.E.

Blessings

141 Pray to learn how to be God's kind of leader: "Heavenly Father, James 1:22 tells me not merely to listen to Your Word—and deceive myself—but to *do* what it says. Help me to hear Your instructions and follow through for the sake of my family and myself."

142 Be ready to serve as a leader. (Don't "escape" by using addictions such as TV, work, drugs, alcohol, etc.)

143 Lead devotions for your wife and/or family. (Make a start by selecting one day each month.)

144 Take initiative this month. (Choose one task you can accomplish as a leader—finances, church involvement, homework help for your children, house repairs, etc.)

145 Let God use the man He created. You have been created in His image (Genesis 1:27)—not in anyone else's image. Believe and *act* on the fact that God has equipped you to be yourself—as a leader.

Comforting

This feeling. She really couldn't identify it, yet it persisted. She was—well, she couldn't really explain it. She just needed something. She felt exhausted and afraid and lonely, yet she really wasn't exhausted, afraid or lonely.

The children were in bed. Her husband had finished the dinner dishes. On the surface, everything seemed fine. But she still had that feeling!

He sat down in the big rocking chair. Suddenly she knew what that feeling meant. She just needed to curl up in his lap in the rocking chair! She needed to be cuddled, to let everything else go and just be in his arms. Safe. Protected. Comforted.

Comforted—that was it. In his arms, in the rocking chair. The perfect place!

What would he say? What would he do? Would he reject her? Would he laugh at her? Would he just want sex, or would he want *her?*

She decided to risk! "Honey, can I curl up in your lap? Would you just hold me and rock me for awhile?"

He didn't say a thing. He just put down his papers and opened his arms. His smile was warm. His hug was firm yet gentle. He rocked her while soaking her intimately with loving looks. Touching her lightly, his index finger followed the curve of her face. Like a slow leak, her internal, unmet needs melted into the quiet of his comfort.

Ever need to be held and rocked? Nearly every woman needs comforting from a man with open arms, a warm smile, a gentle firm hug, loving eyes and hands that caress. Be one!

G.E.

Blessings

146   Become God's comforter for her. "Heavenly Father, 2 Corinthians 1:4 says that You comfort me in all my troubles, so that I can be a comforter to others with the comfort I have received from You. Help me pass this on to _____."

147   Buy a rocking chair and keep it in your bedroom. Make it known that you will hold and comfort her anytime!

148   Buy a warm blanket and keep it in the car. Be the first to bring her comfort at night, on a cold drive home.

149   Keep a tin full of specialty teas, gourmet coffee and cocoa ready for her when she needs comforting. Offer to fix a cup for her!

150   Let her fall asleep in your arms.

Kissing

It was just an old movie. She was just one of those choosy, hard-to-get gals. And the hero was just one of the long list of guys trying to impress her. She wasn't impossible to kiss; she just wasn't impressed by the guys waiting in line!

I'll never forget the scene. A new guy appeared. She looked like she was about as impressed with him as she was with the last ten. And then he kissed her! It was a long, lingering kiss; a gentle, but solid kiss—and she said in sort of out-of-breath way, "Wowwww! I felt that one!"

What was it that made this kiss special? Was it his character or his intent? Without love, you can touch your wife with lust. I wonder if you can also kiss her without love, without meaning in it? And I wonder what makes the difference?

The Bible tells us in Galatians 5:22 that Holy Spirit as our resident Lord has supernatural love as part of His empowering! This supernatural love is there to receive, participate in and release through us. All are acts of exercised faith. Exercised faith means acting on God's promises as truth!

I wonder what would happen if you prayed a little prayer like this:

"Heavenly Father, as an act of exercised faith, in Jesus I am releasing your supernatural love into this kiss!"

Try it!

Perhaps she will say, "Wowwww! I felt that one!"

G.F.

Blessings

151 Kiss the back of her neck.

152 Pick up a classical tape such as Handel's "Water Music Suites" and head for a "make-out session" at a scenic overview or on the beach!

153 Kiss her—and mean it—when you leave each other in the morning. (Give her something to look forward to all day!)

154 Birthday smooches—kiss her once (or more) for each year of her life. (Make growing older something to look forward to!)

155 Turn off every light, and kiss her in the dark.

Holding

It was a hot, humid June day in central Illinois. The cows lay under the shade trees. The temperature was close to ninety-five degrees. It seemed you could hardly breathe. You could feel that something was wrong. Something was going to happen.

My mother came out of the house and gathered us children around her and told us to look to the southwest. There were huge, black, rolling clouds. Below the clouds hung one of the most fearful things we knew, a black swirling funnel cloud roaring like a freight train. It was coming straight for our house!

My mother hurried all of us children into the corner of the basement, under a strong oak table. Huddling us close together, she put her arms around us and prayed that God would spare our house and keep us safe.

I can still feel the earth shake as it did when the tornado passed by our home. I can still hear the deafening roar. The wonderful safety of my mother's arms around us, and the calm voice of her prayer are memories that stay with me, too. Every year I live, the memories grow stronger. I thought she felt like God with skin on. Over the years I have found a safe place in Jesus. I have found a profound calm in prayer in the midst of life's storms. But I still think God in His finest form comes in the shape of fathers and mothers who hold you in their arms and pray.

Perhaps your wife is facing one of life's tornadoes right now. Hold her in your arms and pray. Long after the tornado is past, she will remember you—God with skin on—praying and holding her.

G.E.

Blessings

156 Hold her concerns in your prayers. Actively seek answers for her from God, asking Him to give you specific Scriptures to meet her needs.

157 Hold your temper and your tongue—with help: "Heavenly Father, according to Psalm 141:3, I ask you to set a guard over my mouth, and keep watch over the door of my lips."

158 Hold onto courtesies. Hold her coat as she puts it on—hold out your hand to help her from the car—hold doors open for her!

159 Hold her face in your hands when praying together in bed at night.

160 Hold her warm skin. Sit behind her in a warm bathtub. Light candles, wrapping your arms over and around her—pulling her close to you.

Inviting

Have you ever received an unexpected invitation that just thrilled you? I have. The envelope looked very impressive. It was a business envelope with gold lettering. In the upper left-hand corner it simply said, "President of the United States."

And I said, "Sure, another one of those prank sales pitches." I nearly pitched it into the waste basket. Imagine my surprise when I discovered it was an invitation to the President's Prayer Breakfast. It was signed by the President himself! I was in awe! It was great!

What is so great about an invitation? An invitation is an honor. An invitation says someone values you, someone wants to be with you. An invitation is a risk. You can say "no." Maybe you will say "no," even if it hurts the other person.

Love risks. Love gives invitations. Because of love, you can give invitations. When love is rejected, love just tries another way—another invitation. Love never ends. Neither should invitations!

Give your wife an unexpected invitation today. It will be like a letter engraved in gold from the President, only better. The engraving will be upon the fabric of her heart. It will read, "I love you—always!"

G.F.

Blessings

161 Invite her on a walk—or a short drive to get a cup of coffee or ice cream.

162 Invite her to meet your colleagues at work or your friends from school.

163 Invite her to sit with you outside at night. Take a few minutes to talk about the day, plan tomorrow or just be silent together.

164 Pick up a small package of invitations and envelopes. Fill one out each week for a month, inviting her for a fast-food binge, sporting event, movie or bike ride.

165 Invite her to be with you for important moments. (When your baseball team receives trophies, when a doctor's appointment seems frightening, when your boss honors you for top sales this month.)

Sacrificing

The Potomac. Airliner tragedy. Passenger rescue. The media just called him "the man in the water." What made him great? He decided to be selfless. He decided to sacrifice and help others first. Call him great!

Another Man was beaten beyond recognition. He was forsaken by His friends. His entire being was wracked with pain. What made Him great? He decided to release God's forgiveness, through himself, to His persecutors. He became the ultimate sacrifice. Call Him great!

A third man was one of the most educated people in the first century world. He studied under Gamaliel the elder and was a devout Jew. He had a life-changing encounter with God one day! But what made him great? He decided to link his great mind with God's great character and bless instead of curse. He chose to sacrifice a life of wealth, public honor and prescribed piety. He exercised faith to touch with life instead of crush with death. Call him great!

Want to be a great man? Decide to exercise faith in Christ to be selfless, forgiving and alive with the touch of Christ. Be willing to sacrifice "self."

Maybe she will call *you* "great!"

G.E.

Blessings

166 Surprise her by sacrificing a golf game, workout or Saturday project to take her for a drive. Head for a spot the two of you have talked about visiting!

167 Donate your time for community work or a cause she is particularly interested in.

168 Take the kids for a day, and leave her free to relax.

169 Be willing to sacrifice your pride—especially in public. Has your wife designed, built or fixed something that's usually found in your territory? Give her the credit!

170 Satisfy her sexually. Let her know you strive for her pleasure before your own. (Talk together before the hormones kick in! What would she like? What feels best? Why?)

Desiring

The hot shower pounded on the back of my neck, driving away early-morning tension. "Ahhhhhh." Ecstasy—almost! As I pulled open the shower curtain, my "Ahhhh" changed to "Ohhhh" and my "Ohh-hh" changed to "Wowwwww." There she stood with a cute little smile saying "surprise!" She was wearing the same outfit she was born in!

"Ohhhh, I like your outfit! Wowieeeee"! I stammered.

She cocked her head a bit to the side, kissed me gently and said "I'm wearing it just for you!"

And I had to be at work in thirty minutes! I gave her a little squeeze and murmured in her ear "Honey, you always have and always will have all the electricity to turn on every light in my panel!"

And she said, "Honey, this is exclusive. Just for you. Every kilo-watt of my electricity is just for you, only you. I'm so glad you are my husband—and lover!"

Are physical and sexual affirmations important? They are not only important—they are imperative for security. A warm feeling of secu-rity and well-being spread over me. I was special. She desired me. There was something beautiful and clean and pure, just for me, forever! And it was willfully given! What a gift!

Are you wearing the outfit you were born in just for her? Does she know it is clean and pure and exclusive? Does she know you de-sire her? If she does, some morning soon she may amaze you with the exclamation, "Surprise!"

What a way to get ready for work!

G.F.

70

Blessings

171 Leave a bouquet of flowers in the shower. (With a note that asks if you can join her!)

172 Buy the sexiest lingerie you can find and hide it in her pillowcase. (Tell her how much you desire to see her in it!)

173 Next time she's undressing, tell her how beautiful her body is and how it makes you feel.

174 Leave a note in her car, inviting her for a romantic interlude at lunch! (Find a way to express why you desire her—"You turn me on when you
_____."

175 Keep desire alive—get away from work and house and children! (Take a tip from The Song of Songs 7: 11-12: *Come, my lover, let us go to the countryside, let us spend the night in the villages. Let us go early to the vineyards to see if the vines have budded, if their blossoms have opened, and if the pomegranates are in bloom—there I will give you my love.*)

Emotional
Blessings

Words

During one of the most discouraging times in my life, it was the words of a friend that gave me hope. His words came like refreshing raindrops into my parched soul. My quenched spirit seemed to unfold like a flower turning slowly toward the sun.

The person who said, "Sticks and stones may break my bones but words will never harm," was wrong! Words have tremendous power. Our spirit forms thoughts, and our thoughts form words. The Bible says the tongue has the power of life and death!

Think. Think hard! Have you said words that have hurt your wife? Even if you didn't intend it, were they words of death? Did she flinch or wilt under the impact of your words?

We also have the power to bless with words. My friend's words created hope where there was no hope. Just now, think of words of blessing and words of hope that you can use to touch your wife.

Perhaps her soul is parched. Dry. Touch her with refreshing words like gentle raindrops. Watch her blossom, turn her face toward you and beam with new life!

G.E.

Blessings

176 Thank her often—for meals, housework, encouragement and especially for something she's done for you "beyond the call of duty!" (Bless her with "thank you" at least three times a day!)

177 Invent a code word to use during office parties, family gatherings, social events, etc., that means, "I love you—and let's get outta here!"

178 Give special attention to her voice. What is she saying? Asking? Be committed to answering quickly, with kindness.

179 Use her name when speaking: "Chris, I missed being with you today." Or, "Thanks for helping me last weekend, Julie, I couldn't have done it without you!"

180 Say, "I love you," today—and mean it!

Complimenting

Junior high was rough for me. I was very tall for my age, awkward and insecure. I watched as my friends became interested in boys and had that interest returned. Those girls really began to excel. They were popular. They were good in sports. I, however, didn't seem to shine in any particular area. I was desperate to be good at something—to have someone notice me. I was hungry for compliments.

When it finally came, it wasn't who I expected or what I expected. I was at some family gathering, sitting in the living room, while dad and grandpa watched the Wide World of Sports on TV. Grandpa wasn't much interested in us kids. He didn't ask about school or take us out for ice cream. I think we were a major annoyance to him because we didn't do things right, I wasn't even sure he noticed I was there.

So they watched and I sat. I wasn't particularly into it. Just listening to the hum of announcers at some golf course. The pros whispered. The crowd murmured. I was bored out of my mind.

Getting up to escape outdoors, grandpa's voice stopped me. "Come over here, Jennifer." (What did I do wrong now? I thought.) "You're getting pretty tall, aren't you?" (Don't remind me.) "You know, I bet you'd make a great golfer. You've got the height, strength and a sharp mind. I bet you could play professional golf someday!"

I was stunned. He really seemed to mean it. He was a good golfer—maybe he knew what he was talking about. It was the first time I ever considered my height as an advantage or saw something exciting I could accomplish. It was the only time I remember getting a compliment from grandpa.

Don't let your wife's strengths go unnoticed. Study her. What is she good at? What could she be good at? Compliment her! Those words will last a lifetime.

J.C.

Blessings

181   Compliment her in public. Let people know that you think she's a wonderful wife! (...dancer, lover, cook, teacher, artist, etc.)

182   Notice her progress and successes. Compliment her when she's reached a goal, avoided a bad habit or tried something new. "Heavenly Father, according to Proverbs 25:11, *A word aptly spoken is like apples of gold in settings of silver.* Help me speak those words to my wife!"

183   Appreciate her efforts as a mother. Compliment her affection, loving discipline, patience or creativity with the children.

184   Look at her carefully. Compliment what you see! Beautiful hair? Lovely skin? Sexy legs? Classy outfit? Gorgeous eyes?

185   Acknowledge her qualities as a wife. Compliment her for her wisdom in decision-making, her sexual expression, her commitment to pray for you, her skill in money management, her verbal encouragement or her ability to create a romantic date!

Sharing

I was sixteen years old. It was time for Bible camp. The registration was a whopping sixteen dollars! Not much, right? Wrong! I was one of ten children, and sixteen dollars was a hefty sum. I can remember my parents gathering coins from different places around the house. I was embarrassed to pay my registration with sixteen dollars worth of coins. Little did I realize the sacrifice my parents were making to share this money with me.

At the time of Jesus it was a common thing to sacrifice. For some people, it was common practice to sacrifice one of their children to their god. We see the concept in God's call upon Abraham to sacrifice his son, Isaac. God intervened at this sacrifice, showing us we are not to give up the life of our children, but to give up our self interests.

"How ridiculous!" you say. Yet today, parents are participating in a common sacrifice of their children. Participating in the "sacrifice of passivity," sacrificing their children to the god of television. Sacrificing them to the media, to R-rated and X-rated videos and movies. Sacrificing them to the god of sports. Sacrificing them to the god of prosperity, position and prestige.

My father and mother shared themselves first. They gave each child time—a real sacrifice with ten children. They shared their money for things that counted, right down to their last coins to send me to Bible camp. I was embarrassed by all those coins, but today, I am proud. Proud to have a father who made right sacrifices and was willing to share what he had. I bless my father for his example.

Are you making right sacrifices for your children? If so, they will remember, and they will grow up to bless you! Are you sharing yourself and your time with your wife? If so, she will respond and bless you in return.

G.Ŧ.

Blessings

186 Share in her sense of nostalgia. Make an effort to appreciate her positive memories, the music she likes and her historical perspective.

187 Share your role as leader and "navigator." Allow her to help plan a dream vacation.

188 Be human. Share your grief and fears with her. Let her know it helps you heal.

189 Share your faith. Be willing to tell your children and her what you believe and why you believe it. (Make your relationship with God transparent and real!)

190 Share your focused time. Be willing to put aside the newspaper, turn off the TV or delay a phone call. Convince your wife and children they are first priority—no contest!

Speaking Truth

"Oh, Jill, I wish you could have been at the basketball game last night! It was sooo exciting!"

"Hey, Evie! I wanted to come, but Dave had to work late!"

"Jill, are you sure? I saw Dave at the game. It was during the last quarter."

Jill felt like an elephant had just stepped on her chest. He *lied to me!* And Satan sent a lying spirit. It whispered, "He probably lies all the time!" And she received and accepted the lie. Satan was beginning to fuel a conspiracy to destroy their marriage.

God has a plan to deliver us, to demonstrate himself in and through us and to delight us. Satan has a conspiracy to destroy us. A conspiracy of lies. If Satan can get your wife to believe and internalize a lie, he can put her into developmental arrest. Developmental arrest occurs when a lie is accepted as the standard of truth. It becomes impossible for a person to grow beyond the lie they have accepted.

The development of your marriage can be blocked by internalized lies. The development of your mate's self-esteem can be arrested by internalized lies. A lie is anything that is not truth according to God's Word.

Dave told Jill only part of the truth. His partial truth included a lie. He did work late. But he also attended the last quarter of the basketball game. Satan was quick to use this lie—included within Dave's partial truth—to begin a conspiracy to destroy their marriage.

Yes, Satan has conspired to destroy. However, his only tool is lies. Don't help him! Always tell your wife the whole truth! It's the way to stop Satan's conspiracy to destroy both you and your marriage.

G.E.

Blessings

191   Consider David's words in Psalm 15:

Lord, who may dwell in your sanctuary? Who may live on Your holy hill?

He whose walk is blameless and who does what is righteous, who speaks the truth from his heart and has no slander on his tongue, who does his neighbor no wrong and casts no slur on his fellowman, who despises a vile man but honors those who fear the Lord, who keeps his oath even when it hurts, who lends his money without usury and does not accept a bribe against the innocent. He who does these things will never be shaken.

192   Pray that God will reveal any untruths you need to clear up with your wife.

193   Ask her if there is an area in your marriage where you have repeatedly stretched the truth.

194   Later, write a note asking for her forgiveness, and place it under her pillow. Promise her that she can depend on your honesty.

195   Correct a lie the moment it is spoken.

Supporting

Seaside, Oregon. Long, flat beaches. Unending waves washing in and gliding out. Seagulls. Exquisite kites, and the constant moving of tides. People. Walking. Tanning. Building sand castles. Yet one couple stands out. They were barefoot. She was holding onto his arm with both hands. That was not so unusual, but something else was. Every hundred feet or so they stopped. She leaned hard against him and looked intently into his eyes. The lean was so obvious, it almost seemed as if she backed up a half-step and fell toward him. It was almost as if he needed to brace himself. And it was also obvious they were both enjoying it.

My curiosity and their warm smiles allowed me to ask the question: "You two on your honeymoon?"

They looked at each other and grinned. "Ten years ago we were! We are here reliving old memories and making new!"

I responded, "Well, you sure look happy. Congratulations! I noted something unusual about you. You keep stopping, and when you stop, you lean. You lean hard against him. Do you know that?"

She blushed a bit while leaning even harder and said, "I like to lean against him. My heart, my spirit is so much toward him, I guess my body just sort of naturally follows!"

He chuckled. "Actually, it's because I am such a big pushover! She's just practicing. She is probably about to ask me to buy her a kite or a hot fudge sundae or something!"

"Maybe that too," she grinned. "But really, it's because he is so much man, I can lean against him. He is lean-able."

"Lean-able." It was and is a new word for me. I couldn't get it out of my mind. I still can't. I don't want to. Neither does your wife! Every wife and lover needs a man big enough to be "lean-able."

What does it mean? When the high winds of life blow, you are a tower of strength to lean against. When Satan and evil attack, you are a tower of strength to support her. It means she is never alone! Proverbs 24:5 tells us *a wise man is strong!*

Are you strong enough to support her? Be lean-able!

G.E.

Blessings

196 Express your support for her actions and opinions to others.

197 Support her commitments. (Exercise with her—and let her know you care enough to keep her accountable.)

198 Support her position. (Before arguing with her or questioning her in front of friends or family, give her the benefit of the doubt.)

199 Support her as often as she fails (not just when she succeeds).

200 Support her physically. The Song of Songs 2:6 and 8:3 describe how the husband's left arm is under her head, and his right arm embraces her.

Respecting

Five couples. They've all been friends since high school. Someone is getting the video set up, others are grabbing dessert and finding the best spot to kick back and watch a movie. One of the guys describes a family landscaping project: "More time and money than it's worth, but it wasn't my idea anyway. You know Pam, once she decides on something, I've got to do it—or else!" And in a voice loud enough for everyone to hear, he continued, "It wouldn't be so bad if she helped out, but she's so clumsy, she'd probably wreck everything I've done! Did I tell you what she did last Saturday? Dropped my tackle box on the floor of the garage. Spilled every last piece. Then I had to go clean up after her . . . ."

A company picnic. Everyone is finished with eating, just sitting around talking. Two wives discover that they live close to each other. Lisa describes a shortcut to their house, and hesitates to name one of the streets. "She's always confused!" mocks her husband. "Hey, don't listen to her; she couldn't find her way out of a paper bag!"

A couple drops by to visit friends they haven't seen in several months. Before they're even through the door, Matt tells them how great it is they didn't stop by earlier. "You're lucky you can even see the floor—Lorrie finally cleaned up this pig sty! I don't complain, though, once a year is better than nothing!"

In her heart, each wife moved another five feet away from her husband when these words were spoken.

There is no respect here. Without respect, there is no intimacy. This is character assassination in its most destructive form—disguised by humor.

Consider carefully how you speak about your wife. Are your words flattering, encouraging, respectful? Pray to see her through Christ's eyes. With the intent to bless her, speak to her with words that reveal your respect!

J.C.

Blessings

201 Pray. "Heavenly Father, according to 1 Peter 3:7, as a husband, I need to be considerate as I live with my wife. I must treat her with respect, as a woman with whom I have inherited Your gracious gift of life. By living that way, nothing will hinder my prayers to You."

202 When she is speaking to you, stop what you are doing, look at her and let her know you respect her enough to hear what she is saying.

203 Use a kind tone of voice whenever you speak her name.

204 Treat her friends and relatives with respect. (If not with affection, at least with courtesy.)

205 Respect her opinions and goals. (Tonight, ask her if you have done or said anything unkind—an old joke that isn't really funny—teasing that hurts, etc. Let her know it won't be mentioned again.)

Adoring

There she was! I stood in the midst of a busy auction. Through the crowd of people, I could see her winding her way toward me. At the edge of the auction, she stopped. I carefully watched her eyes sweeping around the crowd. Then her eyes met mine and stopped. My whole world seemed to stop! There was no crowd, no auction, just two eyes—smiling. My insides did those crazy little things that can only be understood by those who have felt it happen!

Was it blessing? Was it love? Or maybe respect? Was it adoration? Whatever it was came through those eyes and that smile! It came banging into my interior like—like wonderful!

That experience was like catching a trophy fish and seeing it glisten — only better. It was like hitting the game-winning homer—only better. It was like the sun bursting through the horizon after a long, dark night—only better. It was just better than—anything! It was something sent from her into my interior that was unlike anything describable. It was just—WOW!

Now I know. It was Jesus! It was God's peace and God's love and God's joy all mixed into one! In the midst of ecstasy, I knew IT was coming through her eyes, and IT was being sent by direct intent! Thirty-six years later, IT is still coming and the thrill is still the same—WOW!

Look into her eyes today with adoration, and with direct intent to bless—create!

I just think she might say, "WOW!"

G.E.

Blessings

206 Do you feel adored? Why or why not? Is it a look she gives you? A touch? Or certain words she speaks only to you? "Research" and try it out on your wife!

207 "Drink to me only with thine eyes . . . ." Ben Jonson wrote that in the seventeenth century. He knew the essence of adoration! Find a moment today to show your wife you adore her—with your eyes!

208 Dedicate a song to her on the radio, and record it for her to hear later.

209 What is it about her that awes you? Her talent? Faith? Looks? Intelligence? Organization? Energy? Tell her—tonight!

210 Look into her eyes and say, "I adore you."

Creating

Nel was attractive. Well-dressed. Her make-up was perfect. Yet, it didn't quite cover the dark rings under her eyes. Her lips were taut. Her neck muscles were rigid. Her presence felt like a tightly wound spring.

With her eyes lowered, she timidly, yet tersely, began. "I probably should not be here. I have it so good, at least everyone else seems to think so. My husband is a good provider. He comes straight home from work every evening. He attends church with me every Sunday. He agrees with me that I should be a homemaker, discipling our children." As she hesitated for a moment, her eyes began to glass over. Haltingly she continued. "But—he is so—critical. I just cannot do anything good enough! Tears began ruining her make-up. "I'm really beginning to believe I'm not good enough. I just don't measure up!"

Finding fault, criticizing and exposing weaknesses is one of the most practiced exercises in America. It's done in the name of humor. The media are specialists. It may be news, but it is not new! It is just plain old character assassination! It is evil and destructive. It is part of a conspiracy of Satan to destroy relationships—the opposite of God's will which is to bless and delight us!

"I just wish one time he would look into my eyes, hold me tight and say, 'Good job, honey. I'm so glad I married you!' I honestly don't know if he is glad he married me. Sometimes I think I am a curse in his life. Or, if not a curse, a second-rate person."

I asked, "Are you blessing him? Maybe in some small way—each day?"

"I'm trying," she said. "But I'm afraid I'm becoming a re-actor. I re-act instead of act. I don't want to, but his constant critical attitude is wearing me down. I'm not responding well! In fact, I think I'm about to lose it!"

She was wrong about one thing. She was 'responding' normally. I believe women are natural responders. I believe Nel was becoming the result of her husbands thoughts, words and actions. He was creating an environment for her to fail.

What are you creating in your marriage? Think. Before—and after—you speak!

G.E.

Blessings

211   Pray to destroy criticism: "Heavenly Father, Romans 14:13 forbids me to pass judgment on _____, because this becomes a stumbling block for her. Instead, I will love her unconditionally. According to Galatians 5:22, I have an inexhaustible supply of Your love for her." (Help her become a new creation in Christ according to Ephesians 4:22-24.)

212   Words create (Psalm 147-148). Be sure yours have God's best for her in mind. (Create *up* instead of tearing down.)

213   Create an environment at home where she finds wholeness and healing as God intended. (Set strict rules between yourselves and your children. What kind of words and actions will not be tolerated?)

214   Reward her when you notice her creating blessings for you. Thank her, and return the favor!

215   Tonight, ask her what kind of person you are helping to create. Does she need healing?

Encouraging

Shortly after my first magazine article was published, I received seven letters. Each congratulation came from friends and family members. I carefully slipped them into the pages of my journal to read again. I read these letters on days when the computer screen is blank—and my mind matches it—when the sky is flat-gray and I feel the same. Each represents a person who has made a long-term investment in me. Before I had confidence in my abilities, before I reached any goals, they invested encouragement . . . .

—A high school English teacher who propelled me beyond a love for stories and into a realm where study was its own reward. He made Harper Lee's, *To Kill a Mockingbird* spread out wide and full like a travel map, saying I had the insight to find my own way.

—My parents who received news that my college degree would be English, and responded enthusiastically that it reflected my abilities and interests. They backed up what they taught: fulfillment is more important than finances.

—A college professor who became interested in me as a person, and graciously probed beyond my rough essays. Editing solicitously, she offered convincing evidence that I and my writing had value.

—My husband's parents who possess an unwavering vision of my ability to accomplish whatever I attempt—even when I have doubts. Their prayers and phone calls lift me.

—A great aunt who makes me feel treasured. Her own achievements coupled with the sheer volume of her love, kindle and inspire excellence.

—My husband whose kindness seems effortless. Sacrificing comfort and stability, he has empowered me to grasp at a dream. His hope in me has no reservation.

When I step back and see these tremendous encouragers, I want to be more like them. They light up rooms—they illuminate souls. But too often I am selfish with my time. In marriage, there is no room for selfishness. Selfishness destroys one of the few essential elements that sustains love: encouragement. Invest in your wife. Her ability to grasp dreams may lie in your ability to speak encouragement.

J.C.

Blessings

216 Hide encouraging notes or love letters in her lunch bag.

217 Encourage her to build friendships, and make it possible for her to go on a weekend getaway with close friends.

218 Leave a balloon bouquet and encouraging note in her car when you know she's expecting a rough day.

219 Lovingly encourage her to meet goals she has set (exercise, prayer, diet, study, career).

220 Pray with her when she is discouraged. "Heavenly Father, thank you for loving and cherishing _____. According to Romans 15:4-5, Your Word gives her perseverance and encouragement. We ask that promise to become true for her today as she faces a difficult challenge. Thank You for hearing and answering."

Impacting

In three, brief moments, spoken words impacted my life.

Sixteen years old! Enthusiasm and hope whirl in my interior like a syncopated dance. The future lies before me like myriads of unsung melodies. "Mom, I think I'd like to be a doctor!" I grin.

"Oh, Glenn," she replies, "your name is Egli. We are not the teachers, doctors or lawyers. We are just ordinary, hard-working, honest folk."

If a mule had kicked me in the stomach, it could not have hurt more. I was "second rate" and born that way. I didn't have a chance. I was ordinary.

And I was an ordinary, hard-working man until age thirty-five, when a friend introduced me to the Dale Carnegie course. He convinced me I was special, a special person. Extraordinary. Not ordinary. I enrolled full-time in college!

During my senior year, the dean of the college invited my wife and I to dinner. "Glenn, your thirty-page paper on the 'Logos' (Word of God) is excellent. I'd like you to consider doing a doctorate in this area. You have what it takes!"

Fireworks burst in my interior. I was not ordinary; I was special. And not only was I special; I was capable! The words of these three people deeply impacted my life.

You can impact your wife. Tell her she is special. Tell her she is capable. Tell her she has what it takes—not only to light you up, but to light up the world around her!

G.E.

Blessings

221 Pray to impact her as a godly husband. "Heavenly Father, according to Ephesians 5:25-27, I can impact my wife for Your good by loving her as Christ loved the Church—giving myself up for her to make her holy, healing her with Your Word and presenting her with radiant character, holy and blameless!"

222 Impact her with literature. Find an autobiography of someone she admires. Read aloud together. How can you help her achieve similar qualities and experiences?

223 Whose words have impacted you positively? How? Why? Decide to impact your wife in the same way. Highlight her talents. Work to expose hidden abilities. Encourage creative skills.

224 Impact her with love. Verbally express your affection for her. Your continuing faith in her as an exceptional friend and lover.

225 Rent the video, *It's a Wonderful Life*. Remind her why she's loved and valued and irreplaceable. Tell her what the world would have been like without her. How has she changed your life?

Balancing

It was a hot summer Saturday. Soccer day. The sidelines. Parents. Cheering. Encouraging. A father and his two and one-half-year old daughter. He was holding her hand. She was screaming, "Let me gooo!"

And the wise father did! The little girl hesitated in amazement at her new-found freedom. She bent over, banged both hands on her knees a couple times and timidly set out to explore! About this time, the soccer ball came to her side of the field accompanied by big, pounding players. The father's eyes never left the little girl.

With amazing quickness, the little girl ran back to her father, grabbed and circled his leg, and peeked out at the big players. Her "let me go" was gone, but her father was not! He dropped his hand and gently held her head against his leg.

The secret to great marriage and great fatherhood is the ability to "let go" and "hold gently with thoughts, prayers and trust."

Husbands and fathers who are unsure of their standing with Christ, won't let go. They hold on with unfulfilled self-expectations, with perfectionist ideals, even unattainable goals. Sometimes husbands' and fathers' standards of success prevent wives and children from attaining and realizing God's standards!

It is a wise man of God who knows when to "let go" and yet "holds gently in the eyes of thought and prayer." When the "big players" of life attack his wife and children, they grab and circle behind and within and find shelter as he gently holds them in his spirit.

"Let me go" and "hold me gently in your thoughts, prayers, and trust" are the same in "father language." It is a precarious balance!

G.F.

Blessings

226 Balance your chores. Spend thirty minutes each evening during the week, and save two and a half hours for family on Saturday morning.

227 Balance your work schedule. See if you can find a way to earn "comp- time" when you work overtime. (Leave two hours early on Friday, and take your children to an afternoon baseball game or splurge on giant ice cream cones.)

228 Examine the balance in your life between mental, physical, emotional and spiritual elements. Is one over-emphasized or completely neglected? (Ask your wife to help you rearrange priorities!)

229 Look at Proverbs 11:1 and balance your expectations. Find out if the children feel your expectations are too hard to reach—ask them! (Have you under- or over-estimated their abilities?)

230 Does your wife find balance between work and pleasure? What can you do to help?

Freeing

We were soon to be married! She was a Wisconsin Lutheran girl, and I was an Illinois Mennonite young man. The Wisconsin Lutherans got together and had fun dancing polkas, schottische and waltzes—even the jitterbug! The Illinois Mennonites got together and had fun—uhhhhh—eating, I guess, without wine and beer!

From my background, touching girls was rated very close to—if not worse than—stealing, drunkenness and laziness! Dancing was, well, you had to touch girls to do that. Anybody, everybody knew what that led to!

As I came to know this Wisconsin Lutheran girl, I learned first hand what it led to: good, clean, healthy fun! And she learned our Mennonite food was as good as, if not better than, lutefisk!

One night in the near dusk quiet of our home, she put on a record and invited me to dance. My fundamentalist insides said no, but my heart said yes!

Freeing. That's what it was all about. As I experienced her character, I became free to trust and enjoy her expressions of fun. It was pure joy.

Yes, it took time to fully experience the fun stored up in this Wisconsin Lutheran girl. I still dance best in the darkness of our own living room, but dancing with her has been one of the most freeing, fun things of my life!

I wonder what other freeing things might be hidden in this Wisconsin Lutheran girl if I were just more open to them?

I know this; I'm asking God to open my eyes and free me to more—fun!

G.E.

Blessings

231 Ask God to transform rigid traditions in your marriage. Feel freedom to try something new! (A new meal, holiday, music or language.)

232 Seek freedom from stereotypes. Just because your wife has "always done it this way," doesn't mean that she isn't longing to try something different!

233 Encourage your wife and children to try a new way of accomplishing something this week—within safety and reason! (It might not be the way you're used to having the house painted or the clothes ironed, but leave room for creativity!)

234 Think of one thing your wife has always asked you to do—but you've been unwilling to do. (Visiting a church, wearing different clothes, eating eggs for dinner?) Decide whether the reason is truly valid or based on fear!

235 Give your wife the freedom to try something new. (Painting? Sky diving? etc.)

Reassuring

As a small child I remember being awed by the massive cedar tree that stood at the edge of my grandparents' yard. It towered above the house. From my second-story bedroom window there, I could see the lower branches up close. If I pressed my face against the window and looked up, the remaining three-quarters of the cedar tree could be seen just brushing the sky. Definitely *not* climbable.

That tree was a landmark for me. It sheltered my dolls when the wind blew. Its roots made croquet the ultimate challenge. Its fallen needles made a tasty "soup" when mixed with pond water! Whenever grandmother took us for walks, she would always navigate by the cedar. "Who sees our tree?" she would call out when we were still blocks away.

"I spy!" we'd answer, knowing that if we should ever be lost alone, the sight of it would guide us home.

The cedar had a sense of reverence around it. Whenever we admired the tree, grandmother would tell the story of how it came to be in their yard. Grandfather had spotted a seedling along a roadside ditch. Knowing how much my Kansas-born grandmother appreciated trees, he scooped it up into his delivery truck, and brought it home. The little tree, no bigger than his hand, was duly planted and watered, though no one ever thought it would survive. I believe grandmother always thought of it as an enduring kindness—reassurance from a husband who was often too gruff to express his love for her.

God has used trees throughout the Bible as symbols of hope and life. [She] *will be like a tree planted by the water that sends out its roots by the stream.* [She] *does not fear when heat comes; [her] leaves are always green.* [She] *has no worries in a year of drought and never fails to bear fruit* (Jer. 17:8).

Perhaps your wife needs a symbol from you to give her lasting reassurance.

J.C.

Blessings

236 Tell her she's beautiful. (Write it on the bathroom mirror using a bar of soap—it can be the first reassurance she gets in the morning!)

237 Make a cassette tape for her to play in her car. (Tell her five reasons why you are madly in love with her and assure her that there are many more....)

238 Buy two apple trees that rely on each other for pollination. (Plant them next to each other in the yard and remind her that you rely on her and need her.)

239 Make her laugh and reassure her of your feelings. Pick up a box of colored chalk and write "I love you" in giant letters on your driveway or sidewalk. (Make sure she can't miss seeing it when she arrives home!)

240 "Borrow" her wedding ring and have it inscribed with a promise from you. Reassure her that your wedding vows are forever.

Stabilizing

My childhood home was a busy place. I was the seventh of ten children. It was busy, but it was stable!

Mother and dad were like the sunrise and sunset. I didn't wonder if they loved me, I knew they loved each one of us. I could count on them to be the same every day—kind and loving.

One day I noted my high school friend looking as if he was dragging a hundred pound weight. "Hey, why the heavy look?"

"My home went through its usual, weekly tornado last night," he said. "My family revolves around my dad's bad moods. His emotions are always ready to erupt. Last night his anger exploded on my mom. My door was closed, but my heart was not. I just don't know how long mom can take it. My stomach is upset. Every moment I live in fear."

Every morning I could remember, our family ate breakfast together, mom read the Bible, and dad prayed. I can still remember kneeling by our chairs and hearing dad pray. He began every prayer the same, "Our kind heavenly Father. . . ."

And I grew up believing God was our God, and He was kind. You see, dad was kind to mom, and mom was kind to dad in return. There was a stable peace in my heart.

I have a "kind heavenly Father," and I had a "kind earthly father." My earthly father is now in heaven, but his relationship with his "kind heavenly Father" lives on in the hearts of his children!

Are your moods stable? Are your children's hearts hurting behind closed doors, or are they learning peace from a stable father who prays, "Our kind heavenly Father"?

G.E.

Blessings

241 Ask God to show you where you need help in being a stabilizer for your family. Start with one area and make it a habit—such as praying with your wife—practice that habit and it will become a desire!)

242 Seek supernatural abilities as a husband and a father. Qualities that stabilize. "Heavenly Father, according to Psalm 68:19, You daily give me strength, You bear me up, You are my salvation. I praise you!"

243 Together with your wife, give your children consistency. Decide on ten house rules that are not to be broken—and definite consequences if they *are* broken. (Post the list for older children to see!)

244 Create a stable environment. Let each child know when they must go to bed, what chores they must do and what privileges they have earned. No surprises or "maybes."

245 Model a stable marriage. Let your children know you often disagree, but show how differences are solved without fighting!

Endearing

"He treats me more like a lawn mower than a lover!" she cried. In this marriage, love was definitely starving—and a husband and wife were starving with it!

I wondered if a love scene I'd seen in a movie might help them—and me! "Whisper sweet little nothings in my ear," the actress said softly.

Pulling her close and looking into her eyes, he said, "You have the most beautiful eyelashes." He stopped for a moment as she blinked those peepers for him. "And your smile! I just love this little dimple!" She acted as if she wanted to crawl inside his skin. He gently stroked her hair as he said, "Your hair is so smoooooth and soft. I just love to bury my face in it softness!"

I had watched and listened to this with amazement. Was he a smooth operator or what? And he had more to say. "Honey, you have the most beautiful neck. I just love to nibble and kiss you on the neck. And that perfume you're wearing! Hmmmmm!"

Of course it was just a movie, but she was eating it up! Putty in his arms, kind of eating it up.

"That is a bunch of 'hokey baloney,'" I thought. Only in the movies. A voice from within me said, "Try it, you have nothing to lose!"

So, I tried whispering sweet little nothings into my wife's ear. It wasn't "hokey baloney" at all. It was endearing!

Endearing. It means, "to win affection." Is affection the response to 'sweet little nothings'? Love needs to be fed in order to be kept alive. Part of the food which keeps love alive and growing is 'sweet little nothings' in a woman's ear. It's called endearment.

Maybe your wife feels more like a lawn mower than a lover! "Sweet little nothings!"—"hokey baloney" or endearment? Try it. There is strong evidence she may respond with, "Tell me again!"

G.E.

Blessings

246 Endear her to you by being spontaneous with affection. Next time you're stopped at a traffic light, lean over and give her a long, hard kiss!

247 Call her sweet, endearing names that only she and you share.

248 Win her affection by treating her with courtesy. (Open doors for her, wait for her to be seated, offer to carry heavy packages.)

249 Make personal cleanliness a priority. Affection comes easier when she is drawn to cuddle with a husband who is sporting clean clothes and a freshly shaven face. (Slipping between the sheets with him after he's just showered is a blessing to her as well!)

250 Be endearing in the bedroom—touch her tenderly and softly describe the feeling of her curves and skin.

Receiving

I was a confident and determined businessman. Yet each day left me feeling uneasy concerning the future. My wife could feel it. "You can do it!" "You are totally sufficient!" "Just dig in and try harder!" "Be independent, stand alone!" I heard songs like, "I did it my way!" Ever hear words like that? They are not Christ's words!

Moses tried to do it, and ended up in a big mess. The Apostle Paul tried it and ended up on the ground. Blind! The disciple, Peter, declared, "I will never." A few days later, he found himself broken. He denied Jesus three times. Moses, the Apostle Paul, and Peter all had their "I can do it myself" broken and burned out of them. Their "I am sufficient" melted into "I need to receive from a supernatural source!"

After twelve years in the business world and four children, I returned to college and seminary. In the business world, I found great pleasure in giving. I realize now there was pride involved, for when I went back to school, I found it very difficult to receive when people offered to help. I was good at giving, but bad at receiving. During ten years in college and seminary, I had to learn humility. Little by little, it became impossible to try harder. Finally, when my resources were almost totally gone, I broke before the Lord and confessed my inadequacy. "I can't do it myself. I need You, Lord. I need help. I need financial help. I need more than human resources. My intellect is not enough. I need You, Lord, and I need your family!"

God didn't want me to try harder. God wanted me to turn to Him, to become conversant with and a participant in the life of Christ and Holy Spirit. As I became receptive to receive in Christ, the impossible became the possible. God didn't do it my way. God did it the right way, His way, the wonderful way. Now, when I check in for duty each day, I ask the Lord to make me His instrument and to provide the resources.

Contrary to what I thought twenty-five years ago, my wife is not uneasy when I am totally dependent on Christ and Holy Spirit. In fact, she is one of the most peaceful people I know. A man who daily receives God's supernatural resources to live God's way will have a wife who is at peace. It's your option!

G.E.

104

Blessings

251 Pray to receive supernatural empowering: "Heavenly Father, according to Luke Romans 6:13b, I offer myself to You in Christ. Through You, I live and act as an instrument of Your righteousness."

252 Receive blessings in prayer from your wife. (Rejecting them is the same as rejecting her.)

253 Learn to receive her forgiveness. According to John 20:21-23, if your stubborn heart prevents her from extending forgiveness to you, your sins are not forgiven. It creates a barrier between you.

254 Allow her to teach you a sport, hobby or skill. Be humble enough to accept her expertise and knowledge.

255 Receive sexual advances from her with pleasure—never let her feel foolish or unwelcome. (Let her know she excites you!)

Renewing

I know a married couple who renew their vows on each anniversary. Not just on their tenth or twenty-fifth, but *every* year. That's unusual enough, but it's not their wedding vows they renew, it's their *dating* vows. Those they've shared with me sound something like this:

> *I always wondered if I'd find someone like you.*
> *I've got to tell you what happened today!*
> *I can't wait for my friends to meet you.*
> *I bought you something!*
> *I'm so happy being with you.*
> *I'll call you the minute I get home.*
> *I just want to stay up all night and talk.*
> *I can't imagine loving anyone else the way I love you.*
> *I can't wait to see you tomorrow.*
> *I'm sorry I did that.*
> *Please don't be upset.*
> *I wish you didn't have to go home tonight.*
> *I miss you.*
> *I wish the weekends didn't end so quickly.*
> *I love the way you kiss me.*
> *I read your letter over and over again.*
> *I want to take you someplace special. I'll love you forever.*

Do you remember what it feels like to be dating? The impractical promises and impulsive decisions? The wild emotions and desires? Somewhere, underneath the calluses that time has left, there is a person who experienced those feelings and had those desires. Why not renew your marriage with some of those first "vows?" She may need to hear that you're still the same guy who made them.

J.Œ.

Blessings

256 Renew your friendship. Invite her to play a sport, go on a hike or watch a movie. (Something that you would normally do with "the guys.")

257 Renew old memories. Recall some of the best times you've had together—and make sure they're still happening!

258 Renew your marriage. Daily commit your relationship to Christ, and spend a few minutes in the morning praying together.

259 Renew old routines. (Change the way you accomplish tasks or change your attitude!)

260 Renew faith. Decide together to memorize one Bible verse each month. (Focus especially on promises God has given in marriage.)

Enjoying

How to bless my wife? I thought I knew. But I had better be sure. So, I started asking wives. I was so amazed by my findings, that I asked a married writer, Jennifer Carrell, to draft several of the texts as well as the practical "blessings" to create this book.

There was one unexpected need that came from wives again and again. "Enjoy me—let me know it!"

I had semi-secretly enjoyed my wife for years and years. I enjoyed watching her mother our children. I enjoyed watching her prepare a meal and be a great hostess. I enjoyed it, but I didn't tell her so as often as I should have.

I enjoyed the way she dressed. I enjoyed the way she undressed. I enjoyed the smell of her powder and perfume in our bathroom. I enjoyed the way she did her hair. I enjoyed watching her comb her hair. And I began to tell her more often!

I enjoyed wrapping my arms around her and placing my face in her hair while she slept. I enjoyed running my fingertips across her face. I enjoyed the fragrance of her body. I enjoyed her total surrender in my arms. I enjoyed her spirit eagerly reaching toward me. But somehow I didn't tell her often enough.

I enjoy her kisses. I enjoy her gentle touch. I enjoy her smile. I enjoy listening to her sing. I love to hear her laugh. Slowly, I am telling her more often!

It is God's first intent for us to know Him and enjoy Him forever. He commands us more than 500 times to praise Him. That's because praise is for our benefit. Praise is a natural response to knowing and enjoying God.

Husbands, it is for our benefit to enjoy our wives. No wonder one of our wifes' greatest needs is to enjoy her and tell her so. It will bring her glory and fulfillment to her husband. Enjoy her and tell her so. It's God's idea!

G.E.

Blessings

261 Enjoy her talents. Watch with pleasure as she paints a beautiful watercolor. Just sit and listen to her play the piano. (Make it important enough that you can drop whatever you are doing, just to enjoy her!)

262 Enjoy her sense of humor. Laugh at her jokes—and pass them on, letting her know they were worth remembering!

263 Smile at her often. Catch her eye and smile at her during a party—make it clear to everyone (and her especially) that you enjoy just being with her.

264 Sleep in with her one morning this weekend. Enjoy the feel of her body against you—let her know you're satisfied just feeling her close!

265 Hold her hand while you watch TV. Trace the edges, touch each finger, gently rub the palm. Softly tell her you enjoy knowing that she is willing to trust you with her hand—and with her love.

Affirming

Women! They have walked into my office for the past twenty-three years. Most have said similar things. "I want a man of God! I wish I would have had enough sense before I was married to insist. My husband thinks romance has to do with fondling, and that blessing ends with buying me flowers. I'm emotionally starved. If I had the choice of being anyone in our family, I'd like to be the dog! The dog receives more affirmation, affection and strokes than I do!"

What is the first mark of a 'man of God'? He loves Christ with unswerving confidence. Second, he loves himself—therefore, he can treat his wife as an equal. It's called respect.

Have you ever viewed a particularly beautiful rose and said "Ohhhhhh, wow!"? That is respect! Every woman wants her husband to view her that way. Respect has to do with affirmation—affirming beauty, affirming talent, affirming potential, affirming creativity.

When affirmation grows out of respect, affection grows out of affirmation. Respect, affirmation, and then intimacy.

Intimacy is not the absence of conflict. Christ-centered intimacy is an unexplainable peace and solidarity in the midst of conflict.

Are you respecting your wife? Affirming? Being affectionate? Intimate? Or would she perhaps rather be the family dog?

Whether she barks or cuddles may be up to you! It's your choice.

G.E.

Blessings

266   Jesus says in John 7:24, *Stop judging by mere appearances, and make a right judgment.* (Ask for God's help to see your wife as He sees her. You may be surprised!)

267   Affirm her efforts whether they are "perfect" or not. (Find something positive to say—the habit will grow on you!)

268   Appreciate and affirm her just as she is—and tell her. (There is nothing that feels more cruel than being loved only if you look right, act right and say the right things, ...)

269   Affirm her for at least five qualities that first attracted you to her. Be sure she knows they still do!

270   Affirm her uniqueness. Assure her that no one could replace her as the gift God has given to you. (Tell her that she is precious!)

Feeling

"I feel like I am being taken advantage of!"

"But you have no right to feel that way!"

Have you ever heard that before? If you were the second speaker, you were wrong! Feelings are not right or wrong. Feelings are feelings! And everyone has the right to have feelings. As to whether those feelings are grounded in truth is another topic.

When our feelings are rejected or declared to be wrong, it becomes harder and harder to share with others. People with rejected feelings often internalize their pain and become a walking time bomb. It takes very little to ignite the bomb!

Jesus was very interested in feelings. Remember when the going got tough for Jesus' followers and many left Him? Jesus turned to the disciples and said, *You do not want to go away also, do you?* Jesus cared about their feelings!

Notice that Jesus approached the disciples' feelings with a question. It quieted all their thoughts of wanting to go away. It's a good approach—try it! ("I'm sorry you have those feelings. That must hurt a lot. Can you help me understand why you feel that way?")

What can you do with your wife's uncomfortable feelings? Follow Jesus' example. Put your hands on her shoulders, look into her eyes and say, "Please help me understand why you feel that way." It just might erase all her thoughts of wanting to go away!

G.F.

Blessings

271   Make a point of asking about her day. But don't stop there! Ask what made her feel encouraged, or what made her feel discouraged about that day.

272   What gives her joy? (Classical music? The ocean? Spring flowers? Ice cream? A long walk?) Feelings expand when shared—so join in!

273   Pay attention to how she describes her abilities. Is she struggling to feel capable of a particular task? Pray Hebrews 13:20-21 with her. Assure her that through the blood of Jesus, she is supernaturally equipped with everything she needs to do God's will!

274   Design a coupon that is redeemable for your undivided attention and non-judgmental consideration. The next time she struggles with a difficult decision or painful feelings, she can present the coupon. (Expiration date: NONE!)

275   Sorrow runs deep—so listen for those feelings inside her. Be ears to hear, and arms to wrap around her. Be a voice to pray when she cannot.

Quieting

I noticed she wasn't sleeping. She rolled frequently and her breathing wasn't right. After listening for about ten minutes, I asked, "Honey, is something wrong?" Silence. Then a little sob! I gathered her in my arms and waited as the sobs shook her body.

She began to speak, haltingly, slowly. Measured words. "It's—it's the children. I'm afraid—" She began to cry again.

I said softly, "I'm afraid too, honey."

"I've been praying and—you haven't been praying with me," she said. "Sometimes I feel so alone taking care of the children. And I get so afraid and—upset!"

I cradled her face in my hand and said, "Honey, please forgive me for not being more sensitive. Let's pray together right now."

I prayed and claimed God's promises for our children. I professed that God's Holy Spirit was guiding us as parents. I prayed and released God's peace into us. I prayed for a quietness in our spirit.

I prayed, thanking Jesus that He was a still point in a turning world. I prayed and asked Holy Spirit to give me more sensitivity to my wife's needs. As we finished praying, I made a new commitment to my wife. I committed myself to her to be a quiet, quieting husband, but not a silent one.

Within minutes, she was asleep in my arms.

Quieting. What is it? It is assurance that you are not alone. It is caring. It is sharing—sharing fears. It is mutual prayer profession, participating in God's provision. It is being led beside the still waters. It is comfort in the face of circumstances that look like death. When a wife needs quieting, God's "staff" is often her husband.

If your wife isn't sleeping well, you might ask, "Honey, is something wrong?" Maybe she needs quieting. If she does, Holy Spirit will help you. He is the Author of quiet!

G.E.

Blessings

276 Quiet her fears with prayer. "Heavenly Father, 1 John 4:18 tells us that there is no fear in love. Since You are a God of perfect love, the punishment of fear is destroyed in Your presence. Thank You for bringing peace to _____."

277 Have a "Do Not Disturb" sign designed in beautiful calligraphy. Frame it, and present it to your wife. Anytime it is on her door, she is off-limits to phone calls and interruptions.

278 Give her a quiet place to relax. Buy a hammock and hang it in a peaceful spot. (She has first priority to use it!)

279 Order nature videos accompanied by Vivaldi's *Four Seasons*. Let her soak in quiet, serene views and beautiful music.

280 During a particularly hectic week, take her to a nearby chapel. (Try a local hospital, university, airport, church or retreat center). Pray quietly beside her.

Spiritual
Blessings

Surrendering

He stood before God. Educated. Willing. Strong. Eager. Talented. A singer. A teacher.

And God said, *I need to bring pressure into your life.*

Intellectual pride flared up. "No way! After all, God, I've been in training. I've suffered enough already. God, aren't you looking? I'm righteous—at least, righteous enough. God, I want to serve you. I will work. I will give you everything: my talent, my time, my money, my—my—."

And God said, *This is your Gethsemane—your surrendering!*

And he shouted, "I don't want Gethsemane!—But Your will—not mine—be done."

Success, at least so-called success, faded. Criticism came. Failure. He had a choice. He could go into depression, curse, and quit—or he could go into despair, and cry out.

He cried out, "God!"

And God said, *Yes! Hang in there. I am preparing you!*

"God, please don't kill me," he pleaded.

He replied, *I must.*

"God," he asked, "please, God, renew a right spirit in me!"

And God answered, *OK, now you have surrendered. I want you to enjoy me, to participate in My presence. To soak in my love. I want you to love yourself. Stop trying to do for Me, and start to experience My presence. Take upon you the suffering of My children. Be an instrument of My supernatural presence. Drive away evil. Bring salvation and wholeness.*

And he said—nothing. His spirit was in awe and astonishment. Worshiping!

This is the best blessing you could give her today. A heart and spirit that have been surrendered to God. Quiet. Worshiping!

G.F.

Blessings

281 "Heavenly Father, according to Proverbs 3:5-6, if I surrender my heart to You, trust You, and don't lean on my own understanding, You will make my path straight. Father, this is what I desire. Help me! You are leading me in a right path!"

282 "Heavenly Father, in Jesus I profess that Matthew 11:28-30 is true for me. I am surrendering to You all my weariness and burdens. I cannot handle them alone. I am receiving Your rest. Thank You, Father, for surrounding me with Your gentle and loving Holy Spirit."

283 "Heavenly Father, according to 1 Peter 5:6-7, in Jesus I humble myself. You will lift me up in due time because you care for me. Under the Blood of Jesus, I surrender all my anxiety."

284 "Heavenly Father, according to Romans 6:3-4, I have already been buried with Christ, so that I may walk in newness of life. I have surrendered my old nature, and it has died with Christ. I choose to walk in His new life according to Your Word."

285 "Heavenly Father, according to Proverbs 16:1-3, as I surrender my work to You, my plans will be established. Weigh my spirit. Search me; then, direct me. Thank You."

Forgiving

How could she be so thoughtless? And it wasn't the first time! Her words felt like burning acid flowing into my ears. My head felt like it was filling with boiling steam, creating pressure that could explode at any time! She turned and walked away with an air that seemed to say the words she had just spoken were as important as swatting a fly.

The internal sting within my being slowly turned to revenge—the desire to react with stronger, stinging words! Have you ever felt that way? God instructs us: *Do not repay evil for evil or insult with insult, but with a blessing, because to this you were called so that you may inherit a blessing* (1 Pet. 3:9).

But how can we forgive when our internal being is raging and stinging? Jesus on the cross is our model. In the midst of a sting worse than we can ever experience, He said, *Father,* (YOU) *forgive them!* And Father God released His supernatural forgiveness through Jesus in spite of His feelings. It worked for Jesus, and it will work for you!

Next time you are hurt or sinned against, simply pray: "Heavenly Father, I choose to release *Your* forgiveness to her right now!" And like a leaking balloon, the sting will slowly leave your inner being. It's Jesus' way. The way to blessings!

G.E.

Blessings

286 Pinpoint a struggle she is having—perhaps a need for healing from a particular hurt. Make a date to pray with her to forgive this person. Remind her that God forgives when we cannot—all we must do is ask.

287 Is there a grudge you have against your wife? Do you continually remind her about some hurt she has caused you? Commit to spend thirty minutes together to talk and pray. Extend forgiveness to her in a way that lets her know that the slate is clear between you, and her and God.

288 Write silly lyrics to describe a mistake you've made—and sing your apology to her!

289 After an argument with one of your children, pray together. Pray to forgive that child, and start fresh again tomorrow. (In what way can you support your wife in this situation? Ask her in what way she needs your help!)

290 Wake up twenty minutes early one day this week. Ask God to show you if you have hurt your wife in any way. Share what He reveals as you go to sleep that night. (Ask her for forgiveness—John 20:21-23.)

Blessing

They came walking down the trail together looking like any other couple, except they were holding hands. "Just married?" asked Ranger Tom.

A grin that looked as if it belonged there spread across Roger's face. "Yep," he said. "We were just married! Thirty years ago last Saturday!"

The ranger seemed a bit embarrassed. "Oh, oh—" he stammered. With an equally pleasant smile, Sally said, "I'll bet you are wondering why we are holding hands. Right?"

"Well, I just—well, it's just not exactly normal on the trail."

Roger spoke again. "It's like this, Tom; when we were married thirty years ago, I was convinced I'd married a girl better than myself. So, since then, I have tried to be worthy to be her husband."

"And how did you attempt to be worthy?" queried the ranger.

"That part was and is easy," replied Roger. I just prayed each morning and asked God to show me how to bless her."

The ranger seemed to be intrigued. "Hmm, you bless her every day, huh?"

"And you, lucky lady, what—uhh, how do you respond to this blessing thing?"

"Well," she cocked her head a bit to the side and said sweetly, "You can see I'm holding his hand, can't you?" Laughter! "Actually," she continued, "I felt the same way Roger did when we were married, and I wanted to be worthy, to bless him, it was so easy—like responding."

Ranger Tom put his chin in his hand and mused for a minute. "Would you say blessing each other has been a big factor in your thirty-year marriage?"

Roger just grinned. Sally spoke thoughtfully. "Ranger Tom, hearing Roger pray each morning, responding to his blessings, and trying to be worthy, has given me great respect for him—and I believe respect and intimacy are synonymous." With a twinkle in her eye, she turned to Roger, put her index finger on his nose and said, "We'd better head up the trail and set camp so you can bless me with some of those super trout, and I can bless you with—well, we'll see!"

The ranger grinned and said "Kids, I don't think I can tell you much about the right trail. I think you're already on it!"

G.I.

Blessings

291 Receive blessings in return. "Heavenly Father, according to 1 Peter 3:9, as I release blessings to _____, I inherit blessings. I choose to be a 'blessor' and a blessed one."

292 Bless her with a phone call during the day and tell her you've kept her in your prayers all morning.

293 Bless her spiritually. "Heavenly Father, according to Ephesians 1:3, _____ has been blessed with every spiritual blessing in the heavenly places in Christ. It is true! She has been blessed and is being blessed as she dwells in Christ."

294 Place your hands on her as you go to sleep, praying to release blessings for specific needs she has expressed (strength, patience, peace.)

295 Bless her with gifts. "Heavenly Father, according to Galatians 5:22-26, You have given her every spiritual gift. She receives and acts on them with joy!"

Restoring

I woke up in a panic, my skin was prickling—someone was sitting on the end of my bed! As my eyes adjusted to the half-light of the cabin, I realized it was my roommate. It was 2:00 AM, and she was just sitting there, staring at me. It gave me the creeps!

This was the beginning of our first freshman camp session. We'd corresponded during the spring and met for the first time just two weeks ago. Both of us were feeling transplanted, out of place. We needed friends. But somehow our friendship didn't seem to be growing. I knew next to nothing about her. She didn't share anything with me about her family, now 3,000 miles away. There were no pictures on her bulletin board, no mail or phone calls from anyone. I wondered if we would ever talk. We were simply two separate lives sharing the same cabin.

But tonight, she wanted to talk. What tumbled out in the next hour came in bitter fragments. No tears, just dry, empty eyes. She had been raped by her stepfather. Then her stepbrothers, uncles and teenage neighbors. In the small town where she grew up, her family was known as trash. She was just second-generation trash.

When she was finished, she didn't blame anyone; she just sat there staring at me. I didn't know what to say. I was sick with her hurt. She had been taken apart piece by piece and when I looked at her, I was sure there wasn't much left of the whole person God had created.

As days passed, I tried to talk with her, but she knew I was failing her. I don't think I ever even prayed over her. If I had, I would have realized that God's healing power could restore her in a way my friendship could not. He intended her to reach her full potential, not to slip downward into deeper despair. His Word promises restoration if only we claim those promises as truth.

In what areas does your wife need restoration? By praying according to the Scriptures, you will restore her to God's fullest potential!

J.C.

Blessings

296   Restore her confidence. "Heavenly Father, according to Philippians 1:6, You have begun a good work in _____, and You will continue until the day of Christ Jesus!"

297   Restore your partnership with your wife. Commit yourself to attend church with her regularly. Pass on the gift of faith to your children, together!

298   Restore her security. "Heavenly Father, according to Colossians 3:3, _____ has died to the world and is hidden with Christ in You. Though storms rage in the world, even though she is in the world, she is resting in Your arms. The victory has been won, and the fight is over forever. She is secure."

299   Restore her trust in you. Become dependable. Never promise her anything you don't intend to accomplish.

300   Restore her peace. "Heavenly Father, according to Colossians 1:19-20, through the Blood of Jesus, _____ has your peace."

Sheltering

It was springtime in the heart of the Illinois farmland, with birds singing and bees buzzing. The grader ditches along the gravel road lined by woven wire fences were lush and green with eight inches of new tender grass! It was my task to let our herd of dairy cows feast there. Easy! Just snooze in the warm sun, and heave a rock at the bossies once in a while to turn them around. A perfect place to dream and be great things in my imagination! It was absolute tranquillity!

Absolute tranquillity, that is until the next farm neighbor came putting along in his pick-up truck. Looking a lot like "Gomer," he leaned out the window and said: "Glenn, do you think you will ever amount to anything?" I was shocked; couldn't this guy see I was already great? Why, if he could just see what I was dreaming! He shot me dead with the following words: "There's not much of a market for cow-herders these days!"

Suddenly, my tranquillity and peace and great dreams were replaced by anxiety and apprehension. With just two sentences, he stole my security and my dreams. I hurried to tell my father of the one-sided conversation. Dad put his arm around my shoulder and said, "Son, you already amount to something. You are my son! You will always be something to me. You are someone special!" And I was secure to dream again.

Security is of utmost importance, especially to women. When a woman's security is taken, her self-esteem goes with it. She begins to feel like a rape victim. This is abuse! Fear, anger and hopelessness are soon to follow.

I wonder if your wife feels like she amounts to something? Are you sheltering her with thoughts (words) of security and self-esteem? Does she know each day she is someone special? Satan is attempting to tell her she is not. Maybe even now he is driving up, leaning out the window and saying, "Do you think you will ever amount to anything?"

Put your arm around her shoulder and tell her how much she means to you. She is special, sheltered, and free to dream again!

G.E.

Blessings

301 Shelter her body. Help her feel protected. (Put your arm around her as you cross a busy street. Cover her in your coat when it's windy. Fend off raindrops with your umbrella.)

302 Shelter her from spiritual attack. Before she has a chance to receive cruel words that someone has spoken—lies from Satan—bind him and his lying spirits and release Holy Spirit to fill her.

303 Ensure that her home is a safe shelter. (Are appliances falling apart all the time? Has the roof been repaired? Are mortgage payments and utility bills paid on time?)

304 Shelter her from verbal abuse. Let your children know that disrespect will not be tolerated. Stand up for her!

305 Shelter her heart as you speak to her. "Heavenly Father, I pray according to Psalm 19:14. May the words of my mouth and the meditation of my heart be pleasing in Your sight. May my words be a blessing to _____."

Empowering

Six-foot-two. Blue eyes and a ready smile. A real hunk. Voted All-American. Popular. Girlfriends. Parties. Lots of friends. Everywhere he went, he seemed to be the center of attention.

He had it made. At least that's what everyone seemed to think. Everyone but him, that is. Inside, something was wrong. "Just ignore it," he thought, "it will go away." But it didn't.

Marriage. A great job. Good finances. And that nagging voice inside saying, "Something is wrong!" "It can't be," he thought, "after all, I'm All-American!" All-American what? An All-American loser.

Lost, because he thought his exterior appearance was all he needed. Lost, because his jokes and carefree character kept everyone at a distance. Inside, he was starving for intimacy. Lonely. Afraid. Lost, because he had learned to depend on self and self-abilities. He exercised hard to keep the exterior sharp, but inside, he was dull. A consuming monster called 'failure' crept closer and closer. Panic time!

One day he heard them—just five words: *God's more-than-human abilities!* He was hungry for it. He exercised faith by praying these words: "Lord, in Jesus, give me your 'more-than-human' abilities; make me All-American on the inside."

And God did.

It worked for him. It will work for you, too. Exercising faith means acting on scriptural truth. It means taking God's Word and the promises He's given us, and claiming them for ourselves. His healing promises are in the Bible. We simply need to recognize them and act on them. Pray. God's Word will become true for you internally. It will heal you. It will heal your relationships. Every wife wants an All-American husband—especially on the inside!

G.F.

Blessings

306 "Heavenly Father, according to Revelation 12:11 and 2 Corinthians 10:3-5, I am not a loser. I am a victorious one being led in triumph, in Christ!"

307 "Heavenly Father, according to Hebrews 9:14, through the blood of Jesus, my conscience has been cleansed. I am free from the accusing voices which say I cannot perform well enough. Indeed, I surely cannot. Jesus already did. And, Father, I am free from the voices which say, 'Something is wrong.' Everything is right in Jesus and I choose to worship You."

308 "Heavenly Father, according to Colossians 2:13-15, through the blood of Jesus on the cross, I am free from guilt. I cease my impossible attempt to become right by performance and accept the fact that in Christ, I am all right!"

309 "Heavenly Father, according to Romans 5:9, through the blood of Jesus, I am justified, just-as-if-I'd-never-sinned! I am clean, free, and good! Hallelujah!"

310 "Heavenly Father according to 1 Peter 2:24-25, through the blood of Jesus, I am healed from low self-esteem and the stinging insults of the past. I am healed from the stinging insults of the past. I am useful and usable in Your Kingdom. Have fun in my life doing what pleases You most!"

Guiding

My great-grandmother was an impressive woman. Pioneering on the Kansas plains during the late 1800s, she was determined to be intelligent, capable and independent. My grandmother's stories described how her mother worked oxen in the fields, handled an eight-horse team, repaired fences, baked, sewed, wrote newspaper articles, played the church organ and was certified to teach school. When my great-grandfather first met her, he was understandably awestruck.

Their married life began on a sizable farm, and people often commented that she was a remarkable help to him in running it. On one particular evening, however, it was *she* who needed help.

In the afternoon, she left their farmhouse on foot to visit neighbors several miles away. When the sky grew dark, they offered her a lantern for the trip home. She cut through acres of grain fields, navigating the tall wheat whose heads waved several feet above her own. Time passed, and the cold air clamped down around her. *She should have reached the farm already.* Tired, and becoming frightened, she called out, hoping someone would hear. No answer. Where was she? Whose farm? How far? Suddenly, she heard a faint voice ahead. A shout to the left, and again. It was her husband, William, who was out looking for her. "Mary! Lift the lantern high! Hold it above your head and follow my voice!" And from far across the dark fields, he guided her safely home."

Perhaps your wife is feeling lost in a less tangible way. Is she struggling with a difficult decision, or a painful personal battle? Release divine healing and supernatural wisdom to her through prayer and words of encouragement. This may be just the kind of guidance she needs—and the kind only you can provide through God's marvelous resources.

J.C.

Blessings

311 Help her meet goals. Ask what she hopes to accomplish this week, or this month, or this year. Guide her in designing a practical plan for achieving these goals.

312 Read *The Miracle Worker* together. The ultimate gift of guidance is to bring someone from dependence to a place of independence, as Anne Sullivan so devotedly brought Helen Keller.

313 Pray over her: "Heavenly Father, according to James 1:5, we ask You for wisdom in this situation, knowing that You will give generously to _____ without finding fault."

314 Pick up books at the library that could provide her with needed information and guidance.

315 Pray together: "Heavenly Father, according to Proverbs 16:3, we commit to You whatever we do, knowing that through You, _____'s plans will succeed." (Also, Philippians 4:13 and 19, and Proverbs 3:5-6.)

Uplifting

The sky was clear and blue. The sun was delightfully warm. A gentle breeze was blowing. Ahhhhh!

Then I saw him. He was standing under the giant umbrella of an old oak tree. Huge beef cattle grazed in the background, silhouetting him. He looked to be deep in thought.

I have seen that look often. I call it "fatigue in the human spirit." Too much outflow. Not enough inflow. Too much time for everybody else. Not enough time for self. Too much fighting. Not enough resting. Too much crying. Not enough "Yahoo's!" Nothing uplifting.

Too busy. Too much. Just too much.

Physical fatigue sets in. Decisions become mechanical. Anxiety, better known as 'narrowness of focus,' pushes toward secrecy. Haunting, lonely questions begin to rattle through the mind like drifting autumn leaves. Fear is soon to follow. "What if. . . !"

Jesus said, *Do not be afraid of those who kill the body but cannot kill the soul. Rather, be afraid of one who can destroy both body and soul in hell* (Luke 12:4-5). Jesus goes on to tell us every hair on our head is numbered, and He observes every sparrow that falls. Then He says, . . . *Don't be afraid, you are worth more than many sparrows!*

Are you aware of Satan? Do you know he wants to destroy you, your wife and your marriage? Are you praying? Uplifting? Does your wife know she doesn't need to be afraid? Tell her! If you are too busy, she will soon have "spiritual fatigue"—and yours won't be far behind!

Pray. Uplift. Her "spiritual fatigue" will lift. Warm sun. Gentle breeze. "Ahhhhh"—with a "Yahoo" in it!

G.E.

Blessings

316 Uplift her day in prayer. "Heavenly Father, according to Psalm 68:19, You give _____ daily strength. You bear her up. You are her salvation. We praise You!"

317 Uplift her spirit in prayer. "Heavenly Father, according to Romans 8:10, because Christ is in _____, her spirit is alive with righteousness!"

318 Uplift her body in prayer. "Heavenly Father, according to Isaiah 53:4-5, Jesus bore our griefs, sorrows, sicknesses and pains on the cross. By His stripes, _____ is healed."

319 Uplift her mind in prayer. "Heavenly Father, according to 2 Cor. 10:4-5, the weapons we fight with are divinely powerful for tearing down strongholds. In Christ, _____ is equipped to take every thought captive and make it obedient to Christ. Our weapons are God's Words in the Holy Scriptures."

320 Uplift her sleep in prayer. "Heavenly Father, according to John 10:27-30, You and Jesus are one. You are greater than all. No one shall ever snatch _____ from Your protection and care. Thank you for this precious promise. We trust in You to keep it."

Praying

The alarm blared into my right ear, and as usual, I could feel the pit of my stomach churn and every muscle tense. It was Monday, 4:00 AM.

Several years ago, every morning started like this. I dreaded getting up and going to work. I dreaded the thought of failing in some way. In my mind I imagined mistakes I would make, clients who would be angry, co-workers who would "tease," intending to hurt.

"Carpe diem" was not happening. I never "seized the day"— the day seized me.

In the midst of all this, I tried to pray, but I just felt numb. The ache of failure was overwhelming. One morning, however, I began to heal. I didn't know it then, but God was choosing to heal me through another person. My husband.

At 4:00 AM, he would gently place his hand on my forehead and pray over me. He prayed for peace according to Colossians 1:19-20, and for healing according to 1 Peter 2:24-25. He bound Satan in the name of Jesus Christ, releasing the Blood of Jesus and angels to protect me, and Holy Spirit to stay with me, equipping me with everything I needed to do God's will that day.

Often, I felt physically relaxed. More often, I felt supernatural love from God coming through my husband's prayers. I knew God was keeping His promises, and I knew healing was happening. I just wasn't very patient! That crisis is now in the past, but my husband still blesses and prays over me often—sometimes for no particular reason. It has become a bond between us and a securing strength for me.

Ask your wife how you can pray for her. Tomorrow morning, hold her and pray blessings over her. Then watch God work healing miracles!

J.C.

Blessings

321 Bless and pray over her in the morning: "Heavenly Father, according to Hebrews 13:20-21, through the Blood of Jesus _____ is equipped with everything she needs for doing Your will!"

322 Leave a message on her voice mail at work or on the answering machine at home to remind her you're praying for her.

323 Create a "prayer closet" for her—somewhere in the house where she can have as much quietness and uninterrupted privacy as possible.

324 Use a small, blank book to list her prayer requests. Spend a few minutes with her each week to record additional requests and record answered prayers. (Pray for her often—and tell her!)

325 Bless and pray over her at night: "Heavenly Father, according to Colossians 1:19-20, through the Blood of Jesus _____ has Your peace!

Exercising Faith

It was springtime. The landscape was alive with flowering trees, bushes and millions of flowers. There were whole fields of daffodils and tulips. Yellow. Red. White. Purple. Smooth edges. Crinkled edges. And awesome, fresh fragrance—like a presence. The setting was so real, it felt as if you could just soak in it.

In the midst of such splendor and fragrance, she walked. Her eyes appeared to reflect the deep red of the tulips—betraying a far-offness as if no one was home. Her shoulders drooped. Her speech was faltering and slow.

Like air slowly leaking from a punctured tire, she spoke. "I'm not sure we are going to make it. I'm not sure he loves me anymore."

This woman could be your wife!

Loving is a decision to continually create, to create by participating in and releasing God's character and God's love to each other. C.S. Lewis wrote, "You'll never know the grooves of grace until you dwell in the ruts of routine." The 'grooves of grace' are a matter of long-term focus. If the 'ruts of routine' are negative decisions, if your thought-words don't agree with God-Words, your focus is wrong! Life won't sing. Love dies. Marriage dies.

Do you want springtime in your marriage? Focus to continually exercise faith. Decide to pray, participating in and releasing God's love to your wife. The awesome fragrance of love is like—but better than—beautiful springtime flowers. Her life will begin to sing; she will turn toward you, receiving the words you've exercised in faith. She will soak in God's blessings!

G.F.

Blessings

326 Exercise faith to forgive. "Heavenly Father, according to John 20:21-23, through the Blood of Jesus, I am empowered to release Your forgiveness through me. I decide to release it through me to _____, for anything she has ever done to hurt or wrong me. Right now, forgiveness has gone to her and right now, I receive and release Your forgiveness into myself."

327 Exercise faith for inner healing. "Heavenly Father, according to Heb. 9:14, through the Blood of Jesus _____'s conscience has been cleansed, and Satan can no longer pound her interior with old failures and hurt. Her conscience is truly cleansed!"

328 Exercise faith into transformation. "Heavenly Father, according to 2 Corinthians 3:18, as _____ looks upon Your face, and sees Your glory, she is being transformed into your image!"

329 Exercise faith for a new beginning. "Heavenly Father, according to 2 Corinthians 5:17, we are new creations. Our past is forgiven and erased."

330 Exercise faith in love. "Heavenly Father, according to Galatians 4:22, Your love is within me by means of Holy Spirit. I release Your love to _____. I choose to love her with Your love, regardless of my feelings."

Mercy

It is Father's Day. I'm on an airplane returning from my fortieth class reunion. I had not been back to my childhood community for years.

I had approached my old community feeling like the prodigal son. What if they remembered I was the high school hellion? My eighth grade teacher was coming. She is ninety-three years old. Would she remember telling my class we would "never amount to a hill of beans"? Would I be seen through their eyes as the community's ornery kid?

I sat down beside my precious, old eighth-grade teacher and asked her if she remembered. She smiled. She did! I told her I had been in the ministry for twenty-three years. She said, "I know; I've been watching you! I knew you kids were smart. You were just lazy, and I didn't know how to motivate you." I thanked her for loving us anyway.

When I faced the community at my homecoming, I didn't want justice. I wanted mercy. I talked to friends and old neighbors who had graduated seventy-five years ago. And I found mercy. Time and wisdom mixed together with love had nearly forgotten the 'high school hellion' and embraced the minister prodigal returnee. I was blessed!

We laughed. We remembered. We forgave. We encouraged. We discussed parents. Somehow, we remembered the good, but especially we remembered the merciful. I remembered hard and perfectionist fathers in my home community. I noted the absence of their sons and daughters. I noted the presence of sons and granddaughters of merciful, forgiving fathers!

If you want to be a great husband and father, be merciful. Leave the door of your heart open and the light in your heart on—the light of mercy! When it's reunion time, mercy is better than justice from an old eighth-grade teacher, from a father, and especially from a husband.

G.E.

Blessings

331 Show mercy and concern when her parents or siblings have hurts or needs. Offer to send a card when one of them has experienced a personal loss or trauma.

332 Realize most of her days are long, busy and tiring. Show mercy with kind understanding when you come home in the evening.

333 Be patient with her when you are working together on a project. Extend mercy and compassion when things aren't completed as quickly or as easily as you would like. (Consider—is this an area where she has likely received any training or advice?)

334 Be merciful when she fails. (If she has experienced a heavy disappointment, purchase a necklace with a locket attached. Engrave with "Love never fails," and place a tiny wedding photo inside.

335 Jesus had such tender mercy that He wept for people. Soften your heart enough to cry with her.

Binding

"Nothing! You can't do anything to help me!" I screamed at my husband. "Just leave me alone!"

For nearly a week I had been tormented with thoughts of hopelessness. I felt worthless, a failure. I didn't deserve my husband. My family didn't love me. Friends were only pretending. Images flashed through my mind of driving my car into a wall or off a cliff. Each day I was losing perspective, sensing blackness surrounding me. God seemed further and further from my prayers.

My husband talked to me, trying to understand what was wrong. He kept asking how he could help. In the space of a few short days, a barrier had been formed between us. The more frightened and desperate I became, the greater the distance grew between us. I needed to be rescued, and I didn't think my husband could do it. In a way, that was true. He couldn't do it alone.

I was involved in a spiritual war. What I needed was supernatural intervention. Since that time, I have learned more about my enemy. It isn't my husband, friends, family or myself. It is Satan. His desire is to separate me from love and righteousness, seizing me as I believe his lies, separating me from God. He knows where I am weak and attacks when I am fatigued and out from under the protection of prayer.

I am learning to identify where a message is coming from before I accept it as truth. God speaks in love to convict us of sin, bringing us through cleansing and healing to reach our full potential. Satan speaks in lies to condemn us, bringing us through sin and evil to reach destruction. If I accept God's Word as truth, I am strengthened. If I accept Satan's words, he sends a lying spirit alongside me to further weaken and seize me.

As my husband realized that prayer was his best weapon, he began to bind Satan, releasing God's promises through Holy Spirit to heal me. Has your wife accepted Satan's lies as truth about herself? Begin to fight the real enemy by claiming promises for her based on God's Word. This is supernatural warfare and God has already won!

J.C.

Blessings

336 "Heavenly Father, on behalf of _____ I bind Satan and any of his lying spirits that are trying to condemn her with guilt. She has already confessed those past sins and You have forgiven her. According to Colossians 2:13-15, through the Blood of Jesus Christ, she is free from guilt!"

337 "Heavenly Father, according to 1 Peter 1:18-19, _____ is delivered from any immoral habits that may have been passed on to her by family members or friends. I bind any spirits of envy, bitterness, anger, lust, greed and _____ in the Blood of Jesus Christ. Instead, Your peace, forgiveness, self-control, contentment and grace are released to heal her."

338 "Heavenly Father, according to 1 Corinthians 10:13, _____ will never be tested or tempted too much. Instead, You will either give her power to resist, or You will remove it from her."

339 "Heavenly Father, by Blood of Jesus Christ, I bind any spirit of confusion that attempts to affect _____ 's ability to make decisions. I claim 1 Corinthians 6:3 on her behalf."

340 "Heavenly Father, according to Psalms 37:3-4, _____ has security in You. I bind any evil spirit of anxiety or fear that is plaguing her."

Releasing

During my sophomore year in high school, my father began operating a tree-removal service. My older brother and I were soon designated as 'climbers.' We climbed high into massive trees, swinging around in rope saddles. Somehow, I think we were trying to convince ourselves we were fearless. But I was not fearless!

One particularly cold morning, I was assigned to climb a bare, limbless tree that needed to be roped down, a small section at a time. In order to do this, I had to climb about fifty feet, vertically. I had no 'hooks' for my feet, so I had to climb by hugging the tree like a small bear. About forty feet from the ground was a small stub—a jagged place where a branch had broken off. As I reached the stub, my sweatshirt slipped easily over it. Resting, I lowered a bit of my weight onto it. I glanced thirty feet to my right. I was looking down into the chimney of a three-story house!

Suddenly, fear gripped my inner being like a vise. My insides began to shake almost uncontrollably, and my strength began to fade. What was happening to me? Would I fall and die?

Then—the voice of my brother called out, "Glenn. Glenn! Don't lose it. Gather your strength and slip your sweatshirt off that stub." The rough bark of the tree burned the inside of my arms and knees. With one last burst of energy, I tried to lift myself up. But I could not. I was becoming more and more paralyzed by fear.

My brother didn't criticize me or give me further advice. He simply said, "I'm coming to help you." I listened to his breathing as he quickly climbed below me—until I felt his shoulders underneath my feet.

"Put your feet on my shoulders and lift yourself off that stub. Now, put your rope around the tree above it and tie yourself in." After releasing me, he took my safety rope and gently lowered me to the ground. He truly saved me!

Maybe your wife is paralyzed by fear. Perhaps you think your wife is inexhaustible. She is not! Maybe even now her strength is leaving and she feels trapped—barely hanging on. She doesn't need criticism or advice. She needs release from fear and a strong shoulder—to lean on. Maybe she needs to hear your voice saying, "I'm coming to help you!"

G.E.

Blessings

341 Listen when she expresses fear. Stop and pray for release. "Heavenly Father, through the Blood of Jesus, I release your supernatural healing to affect _____. You don't want her plagued by fear!"

342 Comfort her. Ask, "What makes you fearful? Is there anything I can do to help you feel safe?" (Does her fear come from a spiritual or physical realm?)

343 Release her fear with spiritual warfare. "Heavenly Father, in the name of Jesus, I bind Satan and all his demons on behalf of _____. They have no place in or around her. Instead, they are cast out. Now, the Blood of Jesus protects her and Holy Spirit is released to fill her. Her spirit can now sing!"

344 Take practical action. If her fear stems from lack of safety, a threatening person, or a dangerous task, pray for creative solutions. Make the house and her car safe. (Contact the police for help or ideas.)

345 Destroy every reason for fear. "Heavenly Father, according to Psalms 27:1, the Lord is _____'s light and her salvation. She has no one to fear in Your powerful light."

Acting

It wasn't as if they didn't love each other. Right now, they just didn't like each other much. They sat across the desk from me, filling the room with tension.

She reminded me of an old porcelain faucet—dripping acid. Each of her words seemed to splatter and sizzle in his interior. Burning. Wounding.

His neck stiffened and his teeth clenched tighter.

When he spoke, it was with a cordial, very controlled reaction. He was smiling on the outside, but sizzling on the inside.

What was her problem? She thought it was him. I thought it was reacting versus acting—calculating without God. Calculating without God is *angustia* (Greek: narrowness of focus), and causes anxiety. Marriage without God—without God's character—is like a bearing without grease. There is constant friction. God's righteousness is the lubricant which keeps marriage running smoothly. Acting through God's righteousness prevents human reaction. She was reacting to the absence of God's character in him, reacting with the absence of God's character in herself! Accusation. Blame. Destruction.

What was his problem? He thought it was her. He was also reacting instead of acting. Anger. Indifference. Hatred. Cordial speech with malice in the heart is hypocrisy. Hypocrisy diminishes respect. When respect goes, so does hope. Neither of them liked being this way—they just didn't know how to fix it!

A righteous, godly character comes from acting—not reacting. Both of these people needed to decide to exercise faith based on God's Word. To create and bring into being God's character and power in their lives. That is acting! Reacting has to do with evil. Acting has to do with God. Are you acting?

G.E.

Blessings

346 Pray for yourself. "Heavenly Father, according to Romans 4:23-24, as I continue to exercise faith in You, You will continue to profess (logos) and send righteousness into and through me."

347 Pray for reconciliation. "Heavenly Father, according to Proverbs 17:9, love can be mine by granting forgiveness. I will seek love and not alienation."

348 Pray for your wife. "Heavenly Father, according to Hebrews 3:12-13, I profess that Your words are true for me. I will turn from unfaithing, from depending on circumstances and feelings. I will exercise faith in You, encouraging _____ so that she will not become hardened or deceived by sin."

349 Pray for each other. "Heavenly Father, according to 1 Peter 2:24, through Jesus Christ, _____ has died to sin, now lives in righteousness, and is healed!"

350 Covenant (promise) together to act as these promises gradually come true. Look for righteous character in each other. (Pray to see your wife change through Christ's eyes. Make a date to share what you see!)

Completing

A friend and I were on our way to a birthday party. I should have been in a great mood, but my heart just wasn't in it. For several weeks now, I'd been looking for more writing assignments to supplement my free-lance work. No progress. As my mind churned over possibilities I had not yet tried, my friend began to describe the accomplishments of her amazing roommate.

This woman works as an administrator for a prestigious research lab, and travels all over the country. She organizes conferences, speaks successfully to large groups and still manages to earn a master's degree in her free time. Her social life sounds incredibly vibrant, of course, and she manages to entertain guests as a gifted pianist. What doesn't she do? Oh, yes, she paints, too!

I measured myself against her and came up painfully short—I was barely able to help my husband pay bills. Somehow, I was measuring myself as if to say: "I am successful if _____." "I am good if _____." "I am only lovable if _____." And perhaps, "God only loves me if _____."

That night, as I shared all of this with my husband, I watched his face and waited for what he'd say. He didn't give advice or make suggestions. He didn't ridicule me for feeling discouraged. Instead, he simply looked at me and said, "I love you. You don't have to do anything to earn my love or achieve anything to make me love you more. You need to understand that you are complete in Christ."

I needed to hear that—and perhaps your wife does, too. To whom does she compare herself? How does she measure her own value? Make time today to tell her you love her. Tell her she is complete in Christ.

J.C.

Blessings

351 "Heavenly Father, according to Col. 2:13-15, through the Blood of Jesus on the cross, _____can cease the impossible attempt to become right by performance and accept the fact that in Christ she is fully complete!"

352 Together, read *What Color Is Your Parachute?* by Richard Nelson Bolles. (Great information for entering the career world, changing jobs and becoming complete as God intended.)

353 "Heavenly Father, according to Colossians 2:10, in Christ_____has been made complete. In You, she has authority over all principalities and powers of darkness. They have no ability to destroy what You have created."

354 Love her without labels. ("I love you, _____. God truly blessed me with you." Not simply: "I love you because you're pretty" or "because you're a great cook.") She is worthy of your love because Christ has made her complete!

355 "Heavenly Father, You have given me spiritual gifts so that I can bless others with them. According to Galatians 5:22-23, I release them to_____, enabling her to become complete in Christ."

Hoping

We were married on June 22, and her birthday was June 29. At least that is what I thought! We were on our honeymoon. At noon on June 28th, I noticed it wasn't too "honey"-like.

"What is the matter, honey? Did I do something? Did I say something wrong?"

"It is not what you've done. It is what you haven't done! It's my birthday and you didn't even remember! I was hoping . . . ."

I felt terrible. I had broken my new wife's hope. It was honest failure, but it was failure! It is a serious thing to break someone's hope. Why?

I believe hope is part of God's character which He shares with us. It has to do with exercising faith in the future. I believe God watches us with eyes of hope. Hope that we will make right, Christ-like decisions that will allow Holy Spirit to be himself in and through us.

Hope fulfilled is like insurance guaranteeing the future. Hope has to do with confidence. Hope is solid. Hope looks at yesterday and tomorrow and knows everything is "OK."

Hope grows and becomes strong with time and performance. Thirty-six birthdays later, my wife's hope regarding my memory and performance has been restored.

I am praying that her hope in me in every area is strong and growing. How about you? Give her reason to hope today!

G.E.

Blessings

356 "Heavenly Father, I ask for Your hope to bless _____ and me. According to Romans 5:5, Your hope does not disappoint us, because your love is poured into our hearts by Holy Spirit, whom You have given to us."

357 Give her hope in your character. Strive to spend time in prayer to develop the kind of character that God desires.

358 Give her hope in your behavior. Take the next three days to make some small change in your habits or actions (more exercise, keeping appointments on time, less smoking, less time in front of the TV, etc.)

359 Share your hope with her. Find something positive to hope for in your job, with the children or in your marriage. Write them down and share with your wife!

360 Give her hope that your love will last. Make saying "I love you" a part of falling asleep together each night, or waking up together each morning.

Loving

Loving. Love. I thought it was something that would "tap me on the shoulder" one day. But it didn't. I had liked lots of girls. There were several who sort of took my breath away. And then there was Ardis, my wife.

Loving. We walked in the October crispness, kicking leaves and laughing. I looked into her eyes at her inner being and decided to love her. It was an incredible risk. I could be rejected.

Loving. We walked through the Evanston, Illinois, streets near Northwestern University, looking into store windows at gala Valentine arrangements. I decided to love her forever. It was an incredible risk. I could be rejected.

Loving. Four times I sat in the waiting room of hospitals, waiting for my children to be born. They came scrunched up and dirty, but I decided to love them forever, no matter what they did or said. It was an incredible risk. I could be rejected.

Loving. I studied and considered God in Christ. He said in His Word that He was love. He said if I reached out to Him in Christ I could know His love as a living experience. It was an incredible risk. Perhaps God was not love. Perhaps He would manipulate and use me. Perhaps He would take away all my fun. And, I could even be rejected!

Then one day my father died. My wife came to me and just held me with love. My children came one by one and just quietly put their arms around me and loved me. And God's Holy Spirit loved me with a reality I had never known.

Loving has not been a "tap on the shoulder." It is a calculated decision. A risk. A risk so big that it requires Jesus. Oh, yes, there have been times when I felt my love was rejected. But I have never lost anything except my pride when I've decided to love. Deciding to risk loving in Christ pays great dividends. Loving—it's God's way. Loving is God happening. Decide today and every day to love your wife!

G.E.

Blessings

361 "Heavenly Father, according to Galatians 5:22a, one of the characteristics of Your Holy Spirit living within me is love. When my human love fails, I will love with Your divine, never-ending love continually."

362 Conduct an experiment: Love blindly for one week, leaving any of her flaws or faults in God's care. Show her affection without any sense that she has to earn it. (Ask God to make this a habit!)

363 Love her. Consider her for a moment. Remove everything on the surface—her face, clothing, hair, figure. What is her essence? Her character? What elements set her above and apart from any other woman? Tell her what you have noticed: gentleness, humor, a kind heart, forgiveness.

364 Love her quirks, habits, funny sayings. Let her know you love her uniqueness!

365 Love forever. Where love is, divorce or emotional abandonment cannot exist. Let your vocabulary and actions reflect permanent love: . . . *Whatever is pure, whatever is lovely, whatever is admirable—if anything is excellent or praiseworthy—think about such things* (Philippians 4:8).

Subject Index